L.O.V.E.

Resources by Les and Leslie Parrott

Books

Becoming Soul Mates
The Complete Guide to Marriage Mentoring
Getting Ready for the Wedding
I Love You More (and workbooks)
Just the Two of Us
L.O.V.E. (and workbooks)
Love Is . . .
The Love List
Love Talk (and workbooks)
Meditations on Proverbs for Couples
The Parent You Want to Be
Pillow Talk
Questions Couples Ask
Relationships (and workbook)
Saving Your Marriage Before It Starts (and workbooks)
Saving Your Second Marriage Before It Starts (and workbooks)
Trading Places (and workbooks)
51 Creative Ideas for Marriage Mentors

Video Curriculum — ZondervanGroupware®

Complete Resource Kit for Marriage Mentoring
I Love You More
Love Talk
Saving Your Marriage Before It Starts

Audio

Love Talk
Saving Your Marriage Before It Starts
Saving Your Second Marriage Before It Starts

Books by Les Parrott

The Control Freak
Crazy Good Sex
Helping Your Struggling Teenager
High Maintenance Relationships
The Life You Want Your Kids to Live
Seven Secrets of a Healthy Dating Relationship
Shoulda, Coulda, Woulda
Once Upon a Family
3 Seconds
25 Ways to Win with People (coauthored with John Maxwell)
Love the Life You Live (coauthored with Neil Clark Warren)

Books by Leslie Parrott

The First Drop of Rain
If You Ever Needed Friends, It's Now
You Matter More Than You Think
God Loves You Nose to Toes (children's book)
Marshmallow Clouds (children's book)

L.O.V.E.

Putting Your Love Styles to Work for You

DRS. LES & LESLIE
PARROTT

ZONDERVAN®

ZONDERVAN.com/
AUTHORTRACKER
follow your favorite authors

ZONDERVAN

L.O.V.E.
Copyright © 2009 by The Foundation for Healthy Relationships

This title is also available as a Zondervan ebook. Visit www.zondervan.com/ebooks.

This title is also available in a Zondervan audio edition. Visit www.zondervan.fm.

Requests for information should be addressed to:
Zondervan, *Grand Rapids, Michigan 49530*

Library of Congress Cataloging-in-Publication Data

Parrott, Les.
    L.O.V.E. : putting your love styles to work for you / Les and Leslie Parrott.
      p. cm.
    Includes bibliographical references.
    ISBN 978-0-310-27247-2
    1. Marriage — Religious aspects — Christianity. 2. Personality — Religious
aspects — Christianity. 3. Man-woman relationships — Religious aspects —
Christianity. I. Parrott, Leslie L., 1964 – II. Title.
    BV835.P36 2009
    248.8'44 — dc22
                                                    2009032622

Published in association with Yates & Yates, www.yates2.com.

Interior design: Matthew Van Zoneren

Printed in the United States of America

9 10 11 12 13 14 15 • 22 21 20 19 18 17 16 15 14 13 12 11 10 9 8 7 6 5 4 3 2 1

To Mark and Stephanie Cole.
May you enjoy all that L.O.V.E. has to offer
(we have a hunch you already do).

CONTENTS

Love Style, n. [lûv stîl]: The way in which your personality is designed to give and receive love.

HOW TO LOVE LIKE YOU MEAN IT

Do everything in love.
1 Corinthians 16:14

YOU WOULD HAVE thought our two little boys, ten and five, would have been more impressed. Here we were, on a beautiful sunny day, standing on the steps outside Mirabell Palace in Salzburg, Austria—the exact spot where Julie Andrews filmed the memorable "Do-Re-Mi" scene with the von Trapp children in the celebrated movie *The Sound of Music.*

"Boys," I (Leslie) said with excitement, "do you remember that scene? Remember how they all jumped on these steps and—"

"Are we going to see the fort?" John, our ten-year-old, interrupted just as I was about to break into song.

"Yea," little Jackson chimed in. "I want to see the fort."

"Can we go to the fort now?" John asked again.

I suppose you can hardly blame them. Hohensalzburg Fortress towers over Mozart's city. This imposing structure is unmistakable, with its spectacular views of the city and the snowcapped Alps. And to little boys who love the thought of being knights in armor with drawn swords, it's simply irresistible. So we put our singing voices on hold and hummed "Climb Ev'ry Mountain" as we took the inclined railway up the steep hill to tour the great fortress and see all the weapons and armory that fascinate little boys.

It's worth noting that throughout its long history, this nearly thousand-year-old fortress has never been captured or successfully besieged by its enemies. Which is exactly the point. A fortress, after all, is designed to keep you safe and out of harm's way.

In a very real sense, this book is designed to help you build a fortress around your relationship. This book is devoted to keeping your love alive and well. It's dedicated to keeping you safe—safe from the squabbles that inevitably attack every unsuspecting couple, safe from the polarizing opinions that try to pull you apart, safe from the inexplicable moments that make you wonder why you chose to be with each other in the first place.

The word *keep*, when used as a noun, is actually the strong central tower of a fortress. The keep is the most defended area of a castle, containing the most important items for survival during a siege. That's why Christians around the world often conclude their worship service by singing the benediction: "The Lord bless you and keep you" (Num. 6:24). And what we are about to show you in this book will do the same thing for your relationship. We want to show you how to love like you mean it—how to love with your whole heart.

This is not a book of handy-dandy techniques to improve your marriage. We're not going to give you a clever three-step strategy for improving your relationship. Nope. This book goes much deeper than that. This book cuts to the core and gets personal. *Very* personal. This book, in fact, is about *you*.

Of course, we don't know you. But we know that you are unique—that nobody else on the planet is just like you.

And we know the same holds true for your spouse. That's why this book, and its accompanying online assessment, zeros in on each of your personal qualities. More importantly, these resources are designed to help you discover the unique combination of your two personalities and how they create a "Love Style" that will forever stand guard over your marriage. We intend to show you that few things can protect the heart of your love for each other more than understanding how each of you was designed for love.

Before we go much further, however, we want to tell you how this book is structured and what you might do to get the most from it.

Getting the Most from This Book

This is not the typical marriage (or premarriage) book. It's more of a program or an experience directing you through a few proven steps designed to bring you closer together. After reading Part One, "What's a 'Love Style'?" you'll be directed to an optional online assessment and then to the chapter(s) in Part Two, "The Four Love Styles," that pertain specifically to you and your marriage. Whether you choose to take the online assessment or not, you'll find Part Two both applicable and practical. The same occurs in Part Three, "Putting Your Love Styles to Work for You," where you will learn specific and personal strategies for loving each other.

So, you won't necessarily be reading every page of this book, only those pages that have direct relevance to the two of you. If you've ever read one of our books before, then you know that we are highly motivated to provide you with any and every potential resource that fits your needs. Here's what we've put together for you as you discover your personal Love Style:

The Online L.O.V.E. Style Assessment

Since you're reading this book, we know you're eager to understand your own Love Style. Well, we've got a simple online assessment designed to help you do just that. And we'll talk about it in more detail in Chapter 2. But if you're already curious, you'll find it at www.Real Relationships.com. The L.O.V.E. Style Assessment takes less than ten minutes, and it provides you with approximately fifteen pages of personalized information on your unique way of giving and receiving love (plus an online exercise packet to use in exploring it with your spouse). And because you are using it with this book, you are eligible for a special discount price. Simply go to www .RealRelationships.com and enter the word "LOVE" when prompted for your discount.

Reflection and Discussion Questions

Included at the end of each chapter are questions for reflection and discussion. These are expressly designed to help you apply the chapter to your relationship. There are no right or wrong answers. The questions simply provide a springboard to stimulate thought and discussion —ideally with your spouse or even in a small group with other couples.

The Optional His/Her Workbooks

Over the years, we've learned that a little over fifty percent of the couples who read our books enjoy using optional his-and-her workbooks to take the material in each chapter to a more personal level. As with our books *Love Talk, Your Time-Starved Marriage, Trading Places,* and *Saving Your Marriage Before It Starts,* we are providing a set of workbooks—one for him and one for her. They aren't required. They are simply for couples who want to go deeper.

If you choose to use these workbooks, you'll see that we have an exercise or self-test attached to each of the chapters. We'll point you to specific exercises as you complete each of the chapters.

The DVD Kit for Small Groups

One of the best ways to learn and apply material like this is in a small group with other couples. If this fits your style, you'll be glad to know that we have developed a DVD kit that is ideal for this purpose. (Of course, it can be used to augment a couple's personal experience as well.) It contains several sessions and is designed to be engaging and fun for facilitating a group experience.

Also, the his/her workbooks have a section in the back designed to enhance your DVD experience.

Online Answers from Us

If you've ever been to our website, www.RealRelation ships.com, then you know that we have more than 1,000 "video on demand" pieces providing answers to questions couples send us. These are not written responses. They are video replies to real questions from couples like you. You can search them by key term and if you don't find what you're looking for, let us know and we'll follow up with you. By the way, these are all free.

The Most Excellent Way

Nineteenth-century Scottish writer, minister, and professor Henry Drummond began his famous lecture, "The Greatest Thing in the World," with a question: "What is the *summum bonum*—the supreme good?" The year was 1883, and Drummond stood before a classroom of college students: "You have life before you. Once only you can live it. What is the noblest object of desire, the supreme gift to covet?"

The rhetorical question required no reply. Everyone knew the answer: Love. Love is the ultimate good. It lifts us outside ourselves. Love sees beyond the normal range of human vision—over walls of resentment and barriers of betrayal. Love rises above the petty demands and conflicts of life and inspires our spirit to transcend what we are tempted to settle for: decent, but merely mediocre relationships. Love aims higher. Unencumbered by self-absorption, love charms us to reach our ideal. Love allures us with a hint of what might be possible. No question about it. Love is the *summum bonum*—"the most excellent way" (1 Cor. 12:31).

When you love like you mean it, your marriage becomes the safest place on earth. Any couple serious about enjoying all that marriage was designed to provide must become students of love. And there's no better way to understand it at a practical level than to learn your own Love Style.

Les and Leslie Parrott
Seattle, Washington

PART ONE

WHAT'S A "LOVE STYLE"?

THIS SECTION SETS the stage for digging into the details of your specific Love Style. It reveals how your marriage is unique. No two people with your specific combinations of qualities have ever been married before. As a result, we'll make several vitally important points about your personalities and how they shape your marriage.

The second chapter in this introductory section sets you up for taking the online L.O.V.E. Style Assessment. It gives you a solid understanding of how the unseen hardwiring of your unique personality can become tangible by answering two big questions. These questions reveal the starting point of your Love Style.

WHY YOU LOVE THE WAY YOU DO

All weddings are similar, but every marriage is different.

John Berger

"WHY IN THE world wouldn't you want to know this?" Les asked.

"Because some things are better left unknown," I replied.

"You're telling me that if you could have your personal DNA spelled out in detail for you, you wouldn't want to know?" he asked. "I mean, you wouldn't want to know what traits you've inherited and what diseases you are most at risk for?"

"No. Not really."

"I don't get it — information is power. This information puts you in the driver's seat of understanding your own genotype."

> I love being married. It's so great to find that one special person you want to annoy for the rest of your life.
>
> *Rita Rudner*

"Well, for now, I feel more comfortable just being along for the ride."

This animated exchange lasted a good thirty minutes. We had tucked our two little boys into bed, and it was the quiet of the evening. We were sitting in Les's study, when he said with enthusiasm: "Listen to this."

He began reading an article about one of *TIME* magazine's "Inventions of the Year"—a retail DNA test that provides you with an online summary of your own genetic makeup (once you provide them with a saliva sample).

Les was gung-ho, ready to plunk down our hard-earned cash on a spit kit that would tell him whether he was prone to Parkinson's Disease, male-pattern baldness, back pain, restless leg syndrome, and ninety-two other bits of biological information.

Me? Not so much. I'm content not to know—and I made that seemingly bewildering fact known to him.

"That's probably one of the things your DNA report would reveal."

"What?" I asked with genuine curiosity.

"Maybe it would show you why you're not more proactive and curious on these matters," Les said, just partly kidding. "Maybe it would show you why you tend to be more passive and why I'm more proactive."

"That's a report I *would* be interested in."

"What do you mean?"

"I'd like a report that reveals my personality traits and compares them with yours—to show us how our two personalities intermingle to shape our marriage relationship."

It was that conversation that became the catalyst for writing the book you hold in your hands. We'd been researching and studying the topic for years. But in that moment, both of us instantly realized how valuable such an assessment could be, not only to our own relationship but also to so many others. After all, if you could accurately understand how your spouse is hardwired for love, not to mention your own hardwiring, wouldn't it almost instantly curb the number of conflicts you encounter? Of course! Wouldn't it create quicker and easier ways to understand one another and bring you closer together? Absolutely!

That's why we dedicate this first chapter to explaining why you love the way you do.

It's All in Your Genes

We need to tell you up front that we are both psychologists. We've been counseling couples and conducting research on marriage for more than two decades. But never have we seen a sophisticated assessment of how two people's personalities combine to create a personal "Love Style."

Of course, there are numerous personality assessments that are effective for individuals. And there are several very good marriage tests for diagnosing relationship issues. But a thorough integration of both has been sorely missing.[1] That's about to change.

We, along with a team of experts, have dedicated a considerable amount of time and effort to developing a valid and reliable online assessment to accompany this book—the L.O.V.E. Style Assessment. We'll have more to say about that in the next chapter.

At this point, we want you to know why we believe this can be revolutionary for your relationship. You see, your DNA—that molecule found in almost every cell of your body—not only encodes the basic blueprint for your biological traits and predispositions, but also it includes much of the encoding for your basic personality.[2] And your personality is central to your love life. In fact, the fundamental premise of this book is to say: *You love the way you do because of your genetic disposition.*

Allow us to say it another way. Your "Love Style" is a cluster of mostly genetic traits that cause you to love the way you do. Your genes, along with the environment you were raised in, shape your desire to be loved in particular ways.[3] Your genes also shape specific ways you go about loving your spouse. When two people marry and combine their individual genetic makeups, differences are inevitable.[4] No husband and wife, no matter how much they have in common, ever have the same personality. Some of the personality differences are clearly

> Marriage is the alliance of two people, one of whom never remembers birthdays and the other who never forgets.
>
> *Ogden Nash*

evident. Some are so subtle they can baffle even the most astute of couples, leaving them scratching their heads:

"Why would he say that?" a flustered wife wonders.

"How could she feel that way?" a confused husband questions.

Now here's the surprising fact: Humans have about 99.9 percent of our DNA in common. Think about that! This means that only 0.1 percent of each person's DNA is unique.[5] Whether you hail from Algeria or Argentina, Zaire or Zimbabwe, your genetic makeup is strikingly similar to that of every other person on Earth. Your genome and the U.S. president's are 99.9 percent identical. In the famed double helix of our two intertwined DNA strands, only a very small fraction makes us unique from one another. Yet that minuscule proportion is enough to create seeming chasms of dissimilarity, causing consternation for almost every married couple.

Why Your Marriage Is One of a Kind

What is that 0.1 percent difference that makes every person unique? Some call it your temperament. Some call it your nature or your character. Mystics call it your spirit. Whatever you call it, we all have it. Like a fingerprint, that tiny genetic difference makes each one of us totally and completely one of a kind. How? Because we inherit three billion pairs of nucleotides, or chemical bases of genetic information, from our mom and our dad. All unrelated people have approximately one change, or difference, in every thousand pairs of nucleotides. So even a 0.1 percent difference makes 300 million chemical distinctions. And that's a lot!

It's tough to comprehend. Think of it this way. There are more than 300 million differences between your genome and anyone else's, and these 300 million different sources of genetic information make your personality exceptional.

Of course, the same holds true for your spouse. Your marriage brings together two completely unique and special personalities. There has never been a combination like you two before. In all of human history, marriage has never witnessed your inimitable combination of personalities. Your relationship is unprecedented. It is unmatched.

That's why you may have found that what seems to work wonders for another couple doesn't seem to help the two of you much at all. We have some friends who married about the same time we did, almost twenty-five years ago. If you ask them what keeps their marriage strong, they'll tell you that they have learned to never fight.

> There is little difference in people, but that little difference makes a big difference.
>
> *W. Clement Stone*

"We have frank discussions, but we never raise our voices," one of them will say. "We've learned to discipline ourselves, and we always count to ten when that starts to happen."

"You've got to be kidding!" Les counters. "Is that humanly possible in married life?"

"It works for us," they say with a smile.

And it does. They're a very happy couple. But Les and I will be the first to tell you that doesn't jibe with our own married life. Not that we have frequent yelling matches. Not at all. Gratefully, we've learned to curb much of our conflict over the years, but it's had little to do with counting to ten.

> Marriage is an alliance entered into by a man who can't sleep with the window shut, and a woman who can't sleep with the window open.
>
> *George Bernard Shaw*

The point is that every couple is unique. It's what caused German poet Heinrich Heine to liken marriage to "the high sea for which no compass has yet been invented"! Sure, there are universal techniques and strategies that can help nearly every couple. Empathy is a good example. What married relationship couldn't benefit from more of that? But putting a technique or strategy for more empathy into practice for each couple becomes a challenge that hinges on that couple's combined personalities.

When Your "Masks" Come Off

Every autumn semester for many years running, I (Les) have taught a university class called "Personality." You'll find this course in every undergraduate curriculum in every college in the country. It's a standard requirement for psychology majors. Scholars agree that this information is essential to a basic education in the science of psychology.

Leslie and I have come to believe that this information should also be required study for anyone who gets married. Why? Because the course is a study in individual differences. And when you study how people differ from each other, you can't help but understand how these differences can also be used to bring us closer together.

Let's start with a definition: Personality is a set of characteristics held by a person that uniquely influences his or her thinking, motivations, and behaviors.

The word *personality* originates from the Latin *persona*, which means *mask*. Significantly, in the theater of the ancient Latin-speaking world, the mask was not used as a plot device to disguise the identity of a character, but rather was a convention employed to represent or typify that character.

Of course, that's not the case when it comes to love and marriage. Think about the first date the two of you ever had. Maybe you went to a nice dinner. We had ours at the Magic Pan in Kansas City on the famed Plaza. Perhaps you went to a movie, or a concert, played mini golf, or attended a ballgame. You can probably recall what you were wearing, what you had for dinner. You may even recollect what you talked about. And you may be able to conjure up some of the feelings you had on that first date. Why? Because, if you are like most people, you put a lot of energy into it. You worked hard to create a positive impression on this person who eventually became your spouse.

> Chains do not hold a marriage together. It is threads, hundreds of tiny threads, which sew people together through the years. That is what makes a marriage last — more than passion or even sex!
>
> *Simone Signoret*

Even if you decided at the outset that you were just going to be yourself, you couldn't help but feel a bit of pressure to "perform" and be the best *you* possible.

It's commonly believed that nearly everyone wears some sort of a mask on their first few dates. They may wear a mask for some time, wanting to continue the charade of the very best version of themselves. Some would argue that mask wearing may even continue into the first bit of marriage. But sooner or later, the masks come off. The real people — and personalities — are revealed. We each see what the other does when hurt, angry, jealous, annoyed, and so on. It can't be helped. If you are with someone long enough in varying circumstances, you gradually discover the actual person. That's why some say that love is blind, but marriage restores its sight.

> The difficulty with marriage is that we fall in love with a personality, but must live with a character.
>
> *Peter De Vries*

We have a friend, Jim Gwinn, who often tells the engaged couples he's counseling, "Just remember: What is now will be then, only more so." It's his way of saying that whatever you find a bit annoying about your spouse-to-be during your engagement will not disappear after you marry. Quite the opposite! It's safe to say that your beloved is actually tempering that quality, and you won't see its full mani-

> What you are as a single person, you will be as a married person, only to a greater degree. Any negative character trait will be intensified in a marriage relationship, because you will feel free to let your guard down — that person has committed himself to you and you no longer have to worry about scaring him off.
>
> *Josh McDowell*

festation until months from now when you are husband and wife.

If Love Is Blind, What Am I Looking At?

Comedian Bill Cosby said, "For two people in a marriage to live together day after day is unquestionably the one miracle the Vatican has overlooked." He's got a point. Once the masks are fully removed and a couple settles into married life with

> Love is not blind—it sees more, not less. But because it sees more, it is willing to see less.
>
> *Julius Gordon*

their differing personalities, it can seem quite miraculous that the relationship endures year after year.

What may be even more phenomenal is that a marriage cannot only survive, but it can actually thrive in the face of two differing and headstrong personalities that face off day after day. How can this be? Let's take a moment to consider a few important facts about personality that can help us shed some light.

Personalities Can Be Seen

Of course, we can't x-ray a personality, but we *can* observe it. How? We can see it because our personality is evident in our behaviors. We can deduce something, for example, about a person's temperament when we notice that she does very careful research before buying a camera. And we can deduce something about personality when we see him purchase a high-priced gadget on impulse. Our behaviors reveal our personalities. And as Yogi Berra so famously said, "You can observe a lot just by watching." Especially when that "watching" is done around the clock in a marriage.

Our spouse becomes witness to our traits day in and day out. It's almost as if we are on surveillance without ever intending it. The mere time that marriage consumes cannot help but make us keen observers of each others' traits as they become visible in our reactions, our expressions, and our behaviors.

You probably don't need much convincing: Personality can be seen.

Personalities Are God-Given

You can't choose your personality like you choose your wardrobe. Relatively speaking, you have just one personality for life. It is something you are born with. Sure, you can modify portions of your personality. Your response to your environment can cultivate or stifle aspects of it. But by and large, your personality represents your natural traits or tendencies.

Ask any mother who has raised at least two children, and chances are she will tell you that they were different from the beginning. For example, one child may have been very friendly and smiled at everyone; whereas the other was always frightened when strangers were present. Each was born that way.

The point is that your personality is in your genes. It is inborn. It is God-given. It is hardwired. You inherited a distinctive set of traits that is fundamental to your nature.

> Don't try to take on a new personality; it doesn't work.
>
> *Richard M. Nixon*

Surely you've heard your spouse say something like, "That's just not you." If you're on the more introverted side, you might hear that statement after your boss asks you to greet everyone as they enter a social gathering. Your personality just isn't cut out for that. Do you do what your boss asks? You do if you want to keep your job. But it feels awkward. The point is that you *can* behave in a way that does not represent your personality, but it will not be your natural response. And it will always be temporary.

Any number of situations may require that you behave in a way that is not natural for you to act, but when the need has passed, you will

> A successful marriage requires falling in love many times, always with the same person.
> *Mignon McLaughlin*

once again act in a way that represents your true temperament. That's because your personality is innate, crafted individually by God.

Personalities Are Predictable

"I knew you were going to say that." How many times have you and your spouse uttered these words to one another? If you're like most couples married for even a short while, you've come to expect certain reactions and behaviors from your spouse. Why? Because personalities are fundamentally predictable. Thank God!

Can you imagine trying to be married if you never knew what to expect from your spouse? A marriage couldn't survive if behavior was not basically predictable. Imagine if one day your spouse was extremely laid-back and easygoing and then the next day was extremely intense and regimented? You'd be living in chaos. Without relative consistency from your spouse, marriage would be an unbearable rollercoaster ride.

Now, we've all had married moments when we say something like, "I never would have guessed *you* would want to do that!" Even with a relatively consistent set of traits, our personalities make room for a smidge of the unpredictable. And that's not bad. Changing things up on occasion can get us out of boring ruts. But for the most part, you can take comfort in knowing that your spouse's personality (as well as your own) will remain pretty predictable.

Personalities Are Powerful

You've heard people say, "He has a powerful personality." They typically mean that the person is charismatic or maybe even overbearing. Truth be told, everyone's personality is powerful. Why? Because your temperament is an internal force that literally produces urges and drives. It's not an exaggeration to say it produces needs. Like a hungry appetite, your personality's needs must be satisfied.

Your personality drives you. For example, if you are inclined to be energized when you are around other people, if you like to talk and be active with others, you have a powerful force within you that finds ways to get this need met. You may be the last one to leave a party, for example. If someone asked you to explain it, you'd casually say, "I just enjoy being around people." It's such an ingrained and powerful part of you that you barely give it a thought.

Now, if you're rather private in nature and feel more content not being around a lot of people, you'll have an equal internal force that urges you to be less social. You'll look for opportunities to retreat from interactions, even feeling like you need to "recover" from too much social stimulation.

Both inclinations are normal. One is not better than the other. But both are powerful. They represent a highly desirable need in the core of the person. And because the need is so deep, because it is literally tied into the individual's DNA, it can create discontentment, even anger, if it is not fulfilled. Make no mistake, the drives that stem from our personalities can be exceedingly powerful.

But are we helpless to do anything about our personalities? Hardly. Soon, we will show you how to harness the power of your personality — so that you can use it to foster the kind of relationship you long for.

> The goal in marriage is not to think alike, but to think together.
> *Robert C. Dodds*

Personalities Have Strong Points and Weak Points

For you to be at your best, you need to have your personality needs satisfied. For example, your personality may crave a detailed plan with time to think things through — whether it be for a major project at work or an evening out on the town. A thoughtful plan makes you a happy camper. After all, this desire to be attentive and prepared has served you well. Other people have praised you for this ability. But if something or someone (including your spouse) stands in your way of having the time to craft a detailed plan for something you care about, you'll inevitably feel off-kilter. You'll worry. As your anxiety increases, you'll get irritable. Even worse, you'll become overly passive, clamming up when asked for your input.

Or perhaps your personality craves quick results. You're decisive. At work you make decisions quickly, with confidence. You trust your instincts and you shoot from the hip. You certainly don't waste time on small talk. The moment someone starts dragging you down by asking too many questions, or if a system impedes your progress with too much red tape, you're bound to get more forceful. Maybe even boisterous and demanding.

You get the point. When it comes to personalities, your greatest strengths can become your greatest weaknesses. Think of it this way. Your personality represents what is important and highly desirable for you — deep down in your core. Meeting this desire is what your personality is consumed with. You are programmed for getting this need met. And when you don't get this need met, your worst side comes out.

That's why you'll hear married couples say sarcastic things like, "Don't you think you might be overreacting here, just a tad?" Or, "Are you losing your mind?" Or maybe, "Oh, that's good. Blow a gasket because I didn't pick up the dry cleaning." These kinds of caustic comments are lethal to love, but it doesn't stop most of us from using them. After all, we can't understand how our normally contented spouse could suddenly "lose it."

> Love at first sight is easy to understand; it's when two people have been looking at each other for a lifetime that it becomes a miracle.
>
> *Amy Bloom*

Personalities Can Be Improved

French philosopher Albert Camus said, "We continue to shape our personality all of our life." And we do. While the basic hardwiring for our temperament is relatively nonnegotiable, we can choose which aspects of our personality to accentuate or moderate. For example, if you know you tend to be rather opinionated and uninhibited, you can learn to control these tendencies when you need to. Or maybe it's in your DNA to be more subdued and matter-of-fact and you therefore get chided for never showing your emotions. You can learn to counter this a bit when it might be helpful. To use a computer analogy, your personality may be your hardware (the computer terminal), but you determine the software (the program) that makes your personality run.

The point is that all of us can learn to improve our personalities. It basically comes down to developing our natural strengths and controlling our natural weaknesses. Part Two includes some specific rec-ommendations on doing just that for your particular per-sonality profile. For now, we simply want you to know that blaming your personality for your atti-tudes or actions is not an acceptable excuse. You are in the driver's seat of your disposition.

> A long marriage is two people trying to dance a duet and two solos at the same time.
>
> *Anne Taylor Fleming*

You and Your Love Style

By now, you understand that your marriage is the combina-tion of two unique, powerful, and God-given personalities. Each personality brings a combination of strengths and weaknesses to the relationship. The mixture of these two sets of traits and temperaments creates a style of loving that is distinct and exclusive to your marriage. And when you unlock the mysteries of how your two personalities combine—how your two clusters of traits and tempera-ments mix—you discover your com-bined "Love Style."

You love the way you do because of your genetic dispo-sition. But you give and get the love you want when you use

> You will find as you look back upon your life that the moments when you have truly lived are the moments when you have done things in the spirit of love.
>
> *Henry Drummond*

your disposition to maximize your Love Style. The remain-der of this book is dedicated to helping you do just that.

For Reflection and Discussion

1. What do you think about the idea that your personality stems from deep down in your own genetic code? Does this make sense to you? Why or why not?

2. Describe a moment early in your marriage or even in your dating relationship when you began to see your spouse without a particular personality "mask" on to disguise an unattractive trait. What was your reaction?

3. Using your own personality as an example, what evidence can you think of that affirms the idea that your natural temperament is powerful? What internal need or urge must be met for you to feel like you're at your best?

EXERCISE ONE
Exploring Your Personality Masks

As noted in the introduction, each chapter will point you to a specific set of exercises and guided discussions with your spouse in the optional his/her workbooks. This first one primes the pump for exploring your own Love Style. It will show you what is particularly unique and special about your marriage because of the combination of your two personalities. It will also lead you through a fun and nostalgic look at the "masks" you wore in the early days of your relationship and show you what you can learn about yourself today by looking at them. This exercise will also prep you for getting the most from the "five domains of marriage."

UNCOVERING YOUR PERSONAL LOVE STYLE

Love is the only way to grasp another human being in the innermost core of his personality.

Viktor Frankl

YOU MAY FIND this hard to believe, but I bought Leslie a birthday gift and waited twenty years to give it to her. It's true. I bought it just before we got married, wrapped it up, and gave it to her two decades later.

This little gift, small enough to fit in one hand, was wrapped in two sheets of simple notebook paper and taped securely at both ends. On the top, it read: "This gift is not to be opened by Leslie until I say so." The sentence was printed by hand in red ink.

"What's in this little box?" Leslie asked the first time she discovered it. We were unpacking our boxes in our first apartment after being married in Chicago and moving that summer to Los Angeles to attend graduate school.

"That's a secret," I said slyly as I took it from her hands.

"Aren't you going to give me a hint?" she asked playfully.

"You'll find out soon enough," I said as I tucked it into the bottom of a dresser drawer under some sweaters.

The next time the little box emerged, we were moving from L.A. to begin a teaching career at Seattle Pacific University. It tumbled out of a moving box and fell onto the floor of our little loft apartment.

"You've got to be kidding me!" Leslie exclaimed as she saw it for the second time. "I forgot all about this thing. What's in here?"

"You'll find out," I said with a laugh. Truth be told, I'd forgotten about it myself.

"It's been six years," Leslie continued as she shook the little box next to her ear, attempting to get a clue. "It's not very heavy. When do I get to open it?"

I'll be honest, I didn't have a timeframe in mind. I had no plan. When I bought this little gift, I thought it would be something I'd give during that first married year. But it slipped my mind—being stuck in the bottom of a drawer and all.

I took the box from Leslie's clutches and stuck it in the bottom of a desk drawer, thinking I'd bring it out for her next birthday, a few months later.

But the little box stayed in the bottom of that desk drawer, all but forgotten, for another six years. It wasn't until we moved again, this time into our first house, that the conversation was stirred up once more.

"Seriously, how long are you going to keep this before I get to open it?" Leslie pleaded. "The suspense is killing me."

I acted like it was all part of my plan. "You'll get to open it when the time is right."

"It's been twelve years! What time are you waiting for?"

Again, I put it away for safekeeping. I stuck it in the back of one of the drawers of the breakfront in our dining room—a drawer that is rarely opened. And there it sat quietly, for eight more years.

Can you believe it? It had now been nearly twenty years that I'd kept this gift under wraps—literally. I never intended to keep it hidden this long. In fact, I never intended to keep it hidden at all. It just happened because I bought it at the same time I purchased another little gift for Leslie while we were engaged. After all this time, I'd forgotten what was in the box myself.

Then it hit me. The image of that little gift came back to me while we were traveling. We had just flown halfway across the country, from Seattle to Kansas City. From there we rented a car and drove two-and-a-half hours south to Carthage, Missouri. It was nearly midnight, and the next morning we were giving a marriage seminar at a local church.

As we pulled up to the Best Western to check in that night, we noticed a large billboard proclaiming Carthage to be the home of "Precious Moments."

"Hey," Leslie said, "you gave me one of those just before we got married."

She was referring to one of those little porcelain figurines that were popular collectibles in the 1980s.

"You're right," I said slowly, as the memory was coming into focus. And then it dawned on me. I bought the little statue in the college bookstore that spring semester in 1984, and the lady at the cash register suggested I also buy the accompanying keychain of the same figurine. The woman was a collector, and she told me that it would be worth something someday.

Well, I guess I was putting her to the test because I kept the little keychain with original packaging in mint condition, unintentionally, for twenty years!

A couple weeks after returning home from that trip to Carthage, I threw the biggest birthday party Leslie has ever had. And with good reason, because it was her fortieth! It had been months in the planning. I'd purchased magazines and newspapers that came out on February 18, 1964—the day she was born. I also had a couple of other memorable gifts. But that serendipitous trip to Carthage served as a major reminder to finally give Leslie the long-awaited little box wrapped in notebook paper that was hidden in our dining room.

With a couple dozen friends filling our kitchen and family room that evening at the party, Leslie spied the little box among her other presents and went straight for it.

"Hey, everybody!" she exclaimed to the group with excitement. "I've been waiting half my life—literally—to open this little box." She went on to tell the story of its occasional appearances. The anticipation in the room was palpable. Everyone was dying to know what it was. And that's when I felt compelled to give a disclaimer:

"Wait a second, it's not that big of a deal. I just—"

"Sit down and let her open the gift," my friend Doug blurted out to the delight of everyone in the room.

So I did. Everyone was leaning in to see what had been covered up for so long. Leslie carefully opened one end of the wrapping.

"I'm going to keep this paper as a testament to my patience," she said.

Then she carefully slid the box from the wrapping to reveal a cheap little keychain with a tiny Precious Moments figurine dangling on one end.

Leslie burst into laughter. She was laughing so hard she couldn't speak as she held it over her head to show the eager group. Everyone else was a little amused, primarily by Leslie's laughter. But mostly they were confused: *What? He kept a goofy little keychain in a box for twenty years and gave it to her tonight on her fortieth birthday? What kind of a sick marriage does this couple have?*

It didn't really matter what our friends thought. I couldn't contain my own laughter as I watched Leslie reveling in the absurdity of the moment.

"I thought it might be something really meaningful," she said through her laughter, "like a letter you wrote to me from twenty years ago or something. But it's a keychain—a Precious Moments keychain!"

"The cashier told me it might be worth something someday," I said with a straight face.

Leslie burst into laughter again.

"The real gift is finally getting to uncover the secret." Leslie told me after the party. "I'm going to keep this keychain in the box on my desk to remind me of this feeling."

You have to admit, there is something immensely satisfying and pleasurable in finally discovering something you've wanted to know for years. It's what poet Carol Lynn Pearson was getting at on a more profound level when she said, "Heroes take journeys, confront dragons, and finally discover the treasure of their true selves." It's a poetic way of saying that life has its challenges and as you bravely slay each one, you come to understand yourself a bit more in the process.

> He liked to observe emotions; they were like red lanterns strung along the dark unknown of another's personality.
>
> *Ayn Rand*

And that's exactly what we intend to help you do in this chapter. We want to help you find the treasure of your Love Style. It's been hidden inside you for years—under wraps for the most part—and we are about to uncover it.

What's Your Style?

"Papa style." That's what our little boys call it when they're taking a bath and they slick their hair straight back from their foreheads. It's the way my dad, their papa, wore his hair his entire life. He just combed it straight back. No fuss. No muss.

You might say that your Love Style is just as straightforward. We're not going to keep you in suspense or lead you though a tortuous labyrinth to make this discovery. You've already seen from the book's cover and the table of contents that we're going to explore four primary styles, using the acrostic of L.O.V.E.:

L – Leader: The Take-Charge Spouse
O – Optimist: The Encouraging Spouse
V – Validator: The Devoted Spouse
E – Evaluator: The Careful Spouse

And, as promised, we're giving you the opportunity to take a sophisticated online assessment to discover how much of each one of these tendencies seem to come through in your own relational hardwiring. But allow us to introduce the concept by presenting you with two vitally important questions. If you can accurately answer each of them, you'll have a pretty good idea of your fundamental L.O.V.E. Style.

Question #1: Are You Project-Oriented or People-Oriented?

We happen to live about four blocks from the Nordstrom headquarters and flagship department store in downtown Seattle. On more than one occasion we have had the privilege of speaking in the boardroom of this company to some of the executives and employees. As you walk through the various floors of office suites, you can't help but notice the same sign hanging in different places. It says: "The only difference between stores is the way they treat their customers."

Now, if you've done much shopping at Nordstrom, you know exactly what that sign means. You see, most stores advertise the quality of their merchandise or the wide selection of their goods. But not Nordstrom. The difference between Nordstrom and most other stores is that other stores are project-oriented—Nordstrom is people-oriented. Its employees are trained to respond quickly and kindly to customer complaints. As a result, according to business consultant Nancy Austin, "Nordstrom doesn't have customers; it has fans."

Now, you might be saying, "That's all good and well, but there have to be some people in the organization that focus on the bottom line more than the customers." And you're right. These employees don't interface much with the customers. Their job is to focus on product quality and inventory. They look at everything from the way the lights hit a display of shoes to the way sweaters are folded and arranged. They are aware of traffic flow within the store and they know how long a product can sit before being discounted. The fact is, Nordstrom couldn't survive without both groups. No effective organization can. We need both people-oriented and project-oriented individuals.

Our question for you is which camp do *you* fall into? One is not better than the other. Just different. The same can be true in your marriage. While you don't *need* both approaches for your marriage to work, both approaches are valuable.

Research reveals that all of us fall somewhere along this continuum:

Project-Oriented						People-Oriented				
5	4	3	2	1	0	1	2	3	4	5

If you place yourself near the Project-Oriented end of the continuum, you prize getting things done. You love an assignment. You probably live by a to-do list. You're gratified by accomplishment—whether solving a minor problem or moving up in your career. You stay on task and you're probably competitive. Getting a job done, whether big or small, can take priority over other considerations (including people's feelings). In fact, anything that stands in your way of getting the task accomplished will likely become a "distraction." You like concrete objectives. You like to measure your progress. Plainly put, you like to be productive.

If you place yourself near the People-Oriented end of the continuum, you generally value the emotional well-being of others over productivity. You're good at working with people and you're friendly. You get a "feeling" for them early on in a conversation and seem to know just what to say. You're rarely forceful or domineering. You're flexible and adapt easily to other people's situations and attitudes. You're diplomatic. You prize consensus and harmony. You're a team player. Nobody would describe you as a "loner." In short, you're a people-person.

In case you're curious, we are polar opposites on this continuum. Les is "Project-Oriented," often focused on a particular task and typically straight to the point, while Leslie is "People-Oriented," sensitive to others' emotions and striving for harmony.

So we pose the question again: Are you hardwired primarily for projects or for people? Keep in mind that one is not better than the other. You may have qualities from both sides of the continuum. In fact, chances are that you are somewhere in the middle. But if you had to choose a side, which one do you lean into most often? Here's a chart to help you clarify the distinctions between the two.

Project-Oriented	People-Oriented
♥ Driven	♥ Nurturing
♥ Measurable goals	♥ Heartfelt connections
♥ Work from a to-do list	♥ "What to-do list?"
♥ Concentrated and focused	♥ Welcome interruptions
♥ Delay gratification	♥ Procrastinate
♥ Make others feel nervous	♥ Make others feel comfortable
♥ "Fish or cut bait"	♥ "Easy come, easy go"

Question #2: Are You Fast-Paced or Slow-Paced?

On the third Monday of every April since 1897, the world's oldest annual marathon takes place in Boston, Massachusetts. That day, an average of 20,000 registered participants wind through the 26.2 miles of streets to the finish line at Copley Square. And it's there that you'll find, year round, a bronze statue of two animals: a tortoise and a hare.

Of course, they are there to remind everyone of Aesop's legendary fable: One day a hare saw a tortoise walking slowly along and began to laugh and mock him. The hare challenged the tortoise to a race and the tortoise accepted. They agreed on a route and started the race. The hare shot ahead and ran briskly for some time. Then, seeing that he was far ahead of the tortoise, he thought he'd sit under a tree and relax before continuing the race. The hare soon fell asleep. When he awoke, he found that his competitor, crawling slowly but steadily, had already won the race.

The moral of the story? It depends on who you identify with most. If it's the tortoise, you'll say: "Slow and steady wins the race." But if it's the hare, you'll counter: "You snooze, you lose."

Which one are you? The tortoise or the hare? Do you approach your day like a long marathon, slow and steady? Or do you jump into the rat race of your day like it's a sprint to the finish?

Research reveals that all of us fall somewhere along this continuum:

Fast-Paced						Slow-Paced				
5	4	3	2	1	0	1	2	3	4	5

Now, if you place yourself near the fast-paced end of the continuum, you probably live your life with a certain level of urgency. You like to get things done *yesterday!* You don't want to waste time. You're ready to get going. You want to use your time wisely. You often measure success in relationship to speed. When you come home from the grocery store with eight or nine bags to bring into the kitchen from your car, how many trips does it take you? Just one, of course. Why? You put a bag or two on each finger, even if it means suffering a bit of temporary pain, in an effort to avoid a second trip. Like we said, you prize efficiency and speed. You can become impatient more easily than others because your days are packed. You schedule things back-to-back. Others are often amazed by how you can get so much done in such a short time. You run on rocket fuel. In short, you're a fast-paced person.

> If you have anything really valuable to contribute to the world, it will come through the expression of your own personality, that single spark of divinity that sets you off and makes you different from every other living creature.
>
> *Bruce Barton*

If, on the other hand, you find yourself on the slow-paced end of the continuum, you take your time. You don't overschedule. You like to linger. If you don't get something done today, you'll get it done tomorrow—or the next day. Why rush, right? Why let the clock run your life? You take your time. By the way, have you ever heard that, "Slow is smooth, smooth is fast?" It's a military saying. It means that moving fast or rushing is reckless and will likely get you killed. If you move slowly, carefully, and deliberately; however, you are really moving as fast as you can without needlessly increasing the risk of mistakes. If you are slow-paced in general, you see its application to more than military maneuvers. You move more deliberately. You take time to ponder and muse. You are measured and unhurried. Plainly put, you are slow-paced.

We are at the opposite ends of this continuum as well. Leslie is more slow-paced, content not to let the clock dictate her activity, taking time for what matters to her in the moment. Les, on the other hand, is definitely fast-paced, striving for maximum efficiency and racing toward deadlines, ahead of schedule whenever possible.

What do you think? Are you hardwired for a fast pace or slow pace? Again, you could be somewhere in the middle. But if you had to choose a side, which one describes you better? Here's a chart to help you clarify the distinctions between the two.

Fast-Paced	Slow-Paced
♥ Divide and conquer	♥ Unite and concede
♥ Impatient	♥ Patient
♥ Raring to go	♥ Ready to rest
♥ Excited and energetic	♥ Steady and stable
♥ To the point	♥ Round about
♥ "Don't just sit there, do something."	♥ "Think before you act."
♥ "Early bird gets the worm."	♥ "Slow growing trees bear the best fruit."

Putting the Two Questions Together

When you combine your responses to these two questions—considering the dimensions of orientation (project or people) and pace (fast or slow)—you can easily see that you'll fall into one of the following four quadrants:

	Project-Oriented	People-Oriented
Fast-Paced	**Leader** The Take-Charge Spouse	**Optimist** The Encouraging Spouse
Slow-Paced	**Evaluator** The Careful Spouse	**Validator** The Devoted Spouse

It's these four quadrants that help us get a handle on your Love Style. As you can see, if you are Fast-Paced and Project-Oriented, you fall into the "Leader" quadrant, making you a "Take-Charge Spouse." If you're Fast-Paced and People-Oriented, you fall into the "Optimist" quadrant, making you an "Encouraging Spouse." And so on.

Of course, the two questions we posed in this chapter are not the best means for discovering exactly where you might land in these four Love Styles. And truth be told, you are probably at home in more than just one of them — as we'll see in a moment. We posed the two questions here only to help you see the big picture of how the four Love Styles come about. It is the online tool, the L.O.V.E. Style Assessment, which will help you pinpoint precisely your unique and personal Love Style, as well as your partner's.

We'll get to the personal nature of these styles shortly. For now, we are simply presenting the concept. With this in mind, here's a table that will help you compare and contrast some defining characteristics of the four Love Styles:

	L	**O**	**V**	**E**
Title	Leader: The Take-Charge Spouse	Optimist: The Encouraging Spouse	Validator: The Devoted Spouse	Evaluator: The Careful Spouse
Descriptor	Doer	Talker	Watcher	Thinker
Motivator	Power	Popularity	Peace	Perfection
Need	Control	Pleasure	Harmony	Excellence
Fear	Failure	Rejection	Conflict	Mediocrity
Satisfaction	Save Time	Win Approval	Gain Loyalty	Achieve Quality

This gives you a little flavor of the four Love Styles. Of course, we have much more to say about each of them. In fact, in Part Two we devote an entire chapter to each Love Style. We'll look at how people with each Love Style approach marriage — how they are hardwired for love. We'll reveal their unique approaches to communication and conflict. We'll examine how people with each style view sex and intimacy. We'll also talk about the unique approaches they have to free time (a common point of contention in marriage). Most of all, we'll zero in on what people with each style need most from their spouse — and how they too often sabotage the very thing they crave. In short, we're going to show you how to get the kind of love you want and how to give the kind of love your spouse needs. We're going to show you how to enjoy the love you were designed for.

> Only those who respect the personality of others can be of real use to them.
>
> *Albert Schweitzer*

Think Outside the Box

Before we leave this chapter, we need to state this clearly: The point of this book is not to put anyone in a box. We don't intend to "label" you. Neither you nor your spouse are likely to fit neatly and completely into one of these quadrants all of the time. People are far more complex than that. Not all individuals can be characterized by a single style. Many people exhibit a combination of styles. And one more thing. Don't read too much into these quick caricatures of the four styles at this point. You might

> True love is that which ennobles the personality.
>
> *Henri Frederic Amiel*

be thinking from these brief descriptions that one is better than another. But that's not the case. Each of them adds significant value to a marriage. Each of them has strengths and each of them has weaknesses. We are all human, after all. Don't for a minute think that one is necessarily easier to live with than another. We all add value, and we all create challenges. But, as you will soon see, once we understand our personal Love Style and learn the secrets to leveraging it, those challenges diminish. In fact, our capacity to love is compounded.

Taking the L.O.V.E. Style Assessment

Before you move into the next section of this book, we encourage you to go online to www.RealRelationships. com and click the link to take the L.O.V.E. Style Assessment. This assessment will take just ten minutes, and it will provide you with approximately fifteen pages of helpful information about your specific L.O.V.E. Style. Ideally, both you and your spouse would take the assessment individually and then have your profiles with you as you read through the remainder of this book. But you'll also gain much by taking the assessment on your own if your spouse chooses not to take it.

> Personality has power to uplift, power to depress, power to curse, and power to bless.
>
> *Paul Harris*

Of course, you don't have to take the online assessment to benefit from this book, but we believe you'll receive the maximum insight of its personalized message by doing so. It's up to you.

We've worked with our publisher to keep the cost of this softcover book accessible because the online assessment requires a minimal fee. We've also designed it so that, as a reader of this book, you and your spouse will receive a special discount on the L.O.V.E. Style Assessment. Once you are at the website, click the link for the assessment and simply type the word "LOVE" when prompted and you will receive discounted pricing.

If you choose to take the online assessment, you'll also want to take advantage of the exercise packet that accompanies it. This packet is complimentary with the assessment and it is included as a PDF attachment with your personalized report. It is also included as a convenience in the his/her workbooks that accompany this book. It's called "Understanding Your L.O.V.E. Styles as a Couple."

For Reflection and Discussion

1. What do you think of the idea of having a personal Love Style? Does it make sense to you? Why or why not?

2. If someone was to observe you over the past seven days, what evidence would they find to conclude that you are either project-oriented or people-oriented? How do you feel about landing in either of these camps? Do you see one as better than the other? Why?

3. Are you more fast-paced or slow-paced? Would your spouse agree with your conclusion? Why or why not? Be specific.

4. If you have not already taken the online assessment, which one of the four Love Styles do you resonate with most and why? Which one do you predict your spouse will identify with most and why?

EXERCISE TWO
Drilling Down on "The Two Questions"

This optional workbook exercise will have you refining your answers to the two big questions in this chapter—and discussing the various aspects of them with your spouse. It will also give you a more graphic way of looking at your particular Love Style by leading you through a series of mini explorations of your personality and how it reveals the way you most like to be loved and give love.

PART TWO

THE FOUR LOVE STYLES

AT THIS POINT, we will assume that you have taken the online L.O.V.E Style Assessment. You now know which of the four styles best describes you. We are also hopeful that your spouse has done the same thing. However, whether he or she has taken the assessment isn't vital to your progress. You can keep moving forward, and your spouse can eventually catch up.

This section is devoted to taking an in-depth look at each of the four specific Love Styles: Leader, Optimist, Validator, and Evaluator. You may be motivated to move straight to the chapter that describes you most. That's fine. Each of these chapters stands on its own. Feel free to do exactly that. However, we strongly encourage you also to read the chapter that focuses on the Love Style of your spouse. In fact, this is imperative for you to get the greatest value out of this experience.

LEADER: THE TAKE-CHARGE SPOUSE

It is better to have one person working with you than to have three people working for you.

President Dwight D. Eisenhower

WITH A LEADER Love Style, you are Project-Oriented and Fast-Paced. The combination of these two dispositions makes you a spouse who likes to be in charge. Note where you land in the four Love Style quadrants:

We'll begin this chapter by exploring your deepest needs. These are the needs you must have met to function at your optimal level—especially in your marriage. Speaking of your optimal level, we'll move from there to "You at Your Best," looking at the five traits

Project-Oriented	People-Oriented
Leader The Take-Charge Spouse	Optimist The Encouraging Spouse
Evaluator The Careful Spouse	Validator The Devoted Spouse

Fast-Paced

Slow-Paced

that emerge from within you when you are doing well and operating in your groove. Of course, we will also take a look at "You at Your Worst." We'll look at the five traits that come into view when your deeper needs are not being met.

> It is almost impossible in our times to think about love, sex, intimacy, or marriage without thinking about power.
>
> *Michael Vincent Miller*

Next, we'll turn to "How You're Hardwired for Love." In other words, we'll explore how your unique combination of personality traits blends together to create who you are as a spouse and what you are looking for in your relationship.

This will take us to how you function within "The Five Domains of Real-Life Marriage." These include communication, conflict, sex, finances, and free time. We'll take a close look at how you approach each one.

Finally, we'll give you some practical ways to "Better Love Your Spouse." After you understand your own deep needs and how they shape your approach to your marriage, you are poised to become much better at loving your partner at a deeper level.

Before we jump in, we want you to keep in mind that you will likely read something here or there that you don't agree with. In other words, you might think that a particular trait doesn't come close to describing you. That's okay. Don't let that interfere with the content you find helpful. Assuming you've taken the online L.O.V.E. Style Assessment, you already know that your personality is too complex to fit neatly into one box. In all likelihood, you are a combination of Love Styles where one is more dominant than the other. That being the case, we don't expect every description in this chapter to fit you perfectly.

Now, take a deep breath. Keep an open mind. And take your time as you discover your own Love Style.

Your Deepest Needs

As a Take-Charge Spouse, you crave control. It's one of your strongest and deepest needs. Whether you know it or not, you've adopted Frank Sinatra's "My Way" as your personal anthem. In fact, you've adapted the lyrics a bit for your marriage. You're not only singing, "I did it my way," but you've added, "and you'll do it my way too."

Your hardwiring not only propels you down the "My Way" Highway, it also makes you like living in the proverbial "fast lane." You live your life with urgency. You think fast, move fast, and make decisions fast. That's why your spouse sometimes feels a bit like roadkill when he or she isn't keeping up.

Your need for control and speed leads to a third need: conformity. You want your spouse to fall in line and, by all means, not slow you down. In a sense, you want him or her to increase your productivity. Or at the very least, not impede it. It wouldn't hurt, you think to yourself, if your spouse would recognize your extraordinary efforts to be productive.

> What I love about my wife is that she's a really strong-minded, stubborn, fiery woman. I find that sexier than anything else.
>
> *Christian Bale*

There you have it: The compulsion for control, the need for speed, and the call for conformity. When these three needs are being met, you're a happy camper.

The Take-Charge Spouse's Motto:
If it's worth doing—do it now.

You at Your Best

The ancient Greek philosopher Plato said, "Good actions give strength to ourselves and inspire good actions in others." He could have been saying that after observing you. You're a person of action. Here are some of the actions and qualities you embody and inspire:

> Good business leaders create a vision, articulate the vision, passionately own the vision, and relentlessly drive it to completion.
>
> *Jack Welch*

Goal-Oriented

Your activity almost always has a purpose because you are results-oriented by nature. You like to close the loop. Check it off your list. Get things done. As a result, you are hardworking and disciplined. Motivational speaker Jim Rohn says, "Discipline is the bridge between goals and accomplishments." You know exactly what he means.

This admirable quality serves you and your marriage well. You don't wait for something to happen in your relationship. You make it happen. You take initiative. You look for solutions. You get results.

> The difference between a successful person and others is not a lack of strength, not a lack of knowledge, but rather a lack of determination.
>
> *Vince Lombardi*

Focused

Some people can't seem to cut through the clutter. You can. You set your sights on something and beeline straight to it, regardless of distractions. Your focus, compared to others, is something to behold. People are amazed by your productivity because of your ability to zero in on what you are after. That kind of focus is uncommon. And when you decide to focus on your marriage, look out! Nothing can distract you. You'll jump over hurdles and tunnel through troubles. What you put your mind to, you accomplish.

Self-Confident

Walt Disney said that he could not imagine any heights that could not be scaled by a person who knows the secrets of making dreams come true. He said they were found in the "four C's": Curiosity, Confidence, Courage, and Constancy. Disney said the greatest of these is confidence. Well, you've got a lock on that one. You're hardwired for confidence. When you're at your best, your self-confidence inspires and encourages others, including your spouse.

Visionary

You have a picture of your future. You can see it. While others struggle to know exactly where they're headed, you're speeding by them in the passing lane. "Vision is the art of seeing what is invisible to others," said author Jonathan Swift. That's exactly what you see—your future—even when your spouse doesn't quite see it with you. By the way, you're not just dreaming about your future, you're backing it up with hard work, determination, and dedication. In other words, you're not just looking to find your future, you're creating it.

Hardworking

"Plans are only good intentions," said management consultant Peter Drucker, "unless they immediately degenerate into hard work." You understand that. You're always ready to roll up your sleeves and work—not just physically but mentally. The wheels in your workroom are always turning. Your mental engine is always running. Even when you're not working on a project, you're working on a project. You may appear to set it aside, but it stays with you. Within the psychic boiler room of your brain, there is always at least a skeleton crew hard at work. And your diligent work ethic is often applied to your marriage. You work hard and, as a result, you get results.

You at Your Worst

It's true what they say, that our greatest strengths can have a dark side. So let's take a look at yours. When you're at your worst—when your primary needs aren't getting met—you tend to demonstrate the following traits:

Stubborn

Every marriage needs a little give-and-take. Unfortunately, that doesn't always come easily for you. You've got a strong will and can become obstinate. Sometimes you choose to dig in your heels and cling to your position no matter the cost.

> The difference between perseverance and obstinacy is that one often comes from a strong will, and the other from a strong won't.
>
> *Henry Ward Beecher*

That leaves little room for negotiating, which leaves your spouse in the cold. Thankfully, this occurs only occasionally for you, but it happens more with you than it does with other styles.

Insensitive

This may sound harsh, but you have an inclination to put down anyone who doesn't move fast enough or think like you do. This can be the person driving the car in front of you on the road or, of course, it can be your spouse. When pointing out faults doesn't work, you may resort to snide comments or direct insults. Ouch! The point is, you don't easily empathize with your partner's feelings, and you're slow to show compassion. At your worst, you tend to be tactless, rude, and insensitive. Are you cringing yet?

Easily Annoyed

Have you ever noticed how some people have a low threshold for annoyance? Seems the slightest thing can tic them off. It may be that their shirt wasn't ironed right, that they can't find the pen they left on their desk, or that someone left litter in their car. What others shrug off, they take to heart. Well, that's you. You're easily aggravated. It's a weakness fueled by impatience. That's what too often keeps you on edge and makes you irritated. As for your spouse? It makes him or her feel inadequate.

Hot-Tempered

One of the scariest parts of your personality is found when your irritation becomes full-blown anger. Be honest, you've had moments when your anger was on a hair trigger. As a result, you arm yourself with the threat of anger in marriage. Just the possible unleashing of your rage has probably become enough for your spouse to back off in those moments when it begins to flare. Yup, unfortunately, anger for you can become a tool of control.

Domineering

Someone said that love does not dominate, it cultivates, meaning that a loving approach is to create an environment in which other people can become themselves and flourish. You may agree with this sentiment, but you have a tough time living it out.

How many times have you tried to find a solution before you accurately understood the problem? As a Take-Charge Spouse, you are prone to act before you have the facts. Since you are quick to make decisions for yourself, you tend to be quick to make them for your spouse as well. In your bad moments, that can make you heavy-handed, forceful, and sometimes bossy.

> I can't be a wife. I'm not that sort of person. Wives have to compromise all the time.
>
> *Sarah Brightman*

How You're Hardwired to Love

When it comes to your marriage, you tend to treat it like any other project. You have objective goals you want it to reach. You have standards you want it to maintain. You have a tactical plan ready to implement. And you expect positive payoffs. In other words, you have a marriage with a mission.

To keep your marriage "productive," you assess what's needed and give it the attention it requires—especially if a caution light goes off. And once your marriage is in good shape and running smoothly, you then feel freed up to shift to another project.

When Thomas, a Take-Charge Husband, realized his wife was feeling drained and neglected, he zeroed in on the issue and kicked into romance mode with a plan of action. "Honey, we need to have more time for just the two of us. It's been too long. I'm hiring a babysitter this weekend and I'm taking you out—just you and me." Wow! That did the trick. His wife was thrilled. With that problem solved, Thomas shifted gears and put his attention back onto a pressing project at work.

Here's the catch for you as a person who is running fast: To get intentional, you often need to be reminded of your marriage. That may sound silly, but because you operate by a to-do list, you end up neglecting your relationship if something doesn't cause you to stop and focus on it. We probably don't need to tell you that your "reminder" is too often your spouse (which is a drag). But it can be nearly anything else: the news of a friend's marriage turning sour, a movie that hits close to home, a sermon that wakes you up. You name it.

The point is that something needs to grab your attention to get you to focus on your marriage. The good news is that once you see a warning flag, you get intentional immediately. You take action. And you typically get positive results.

You also want to deal with conflict immediately and head-on. But you don't always realize that other styles need time to process conflict and may not want to "get in the ring" to get conflict resolved.

You also know, instinctively, that your marriage has a mission. As a purpose-driven spouse, your visionary abilities cause you to keep the future in mind. That's why you initiate experiences that create memories. You don't just wait for the fun to find you and your marriage, you hunt it down by planning trips and scheduling adventures. Your spouse would never call you a passive stick-in-the-mud. You've always got ideas and dreams that energize your relationship.

> Vision without action is a dream. Action without vision is simply passing the time. Action with vision is making a positive difference.
>
> *Joel Barker*

Valarie got a quizzical look from her husband when she proposed that they write out a marital mission statement. As a Take-Charge Wife, it made perfect sense to her. She had a mission statement for her job. Why not her marriage? Eventually, her husband got on board with the idea, and they've both come to value their shared mission as a couple.

As a Take-Charge Spouse, you express your love by helping your marriage reach goals. You dream about the future, and you create a vision for getting to the place you want your marriage to be. You may have a financial vision to reach a savings goal, for example. You may have a vision for how you'll approach your vacations. You have a vision about raising a family together. Your vision may lead to specific plans, but not necessarily. In other words, you can commit to a vision without understanding the details of how it will be realized. You simply have the confidence that the details will come in time. (Consequently, you are comfortable changing gears throughout your journey.)

> Give us clear vision that we may know where to stand and what to stand for — because unless we stand for something we shall fall for anything.
>
> *Peter Marshall*

By the way, you feel most loved when your spouse gets behind your plans and helps you execute them. You feel loved when your spouse does anything that saves you time and makes you more productive.

The bottom line is that you are hardwired to love by *doing* loving things, by making a positive influence on your relationship through your actions. Once your marriage gets your attention, you quickly assess what's needed and fashion a plan to make your marriage the best it can be — as swiftly as possible.

How the Take-Charge Spouse Defines Love
Love is . . . being intentional and active
about building our future together.

You and the Five Domains of Real-Life Marriage

Every marriage, regardless of its stage, has specific domains that can become sticking points between a husband and wife. This is especially true for couples who have not explored how their personal Love Styles impact and shape each one of these domains. These include: communication, conflict, sex, finances, and free time.

Here's how you approach each of them.

Your Approach to Communication

Direct and to the point. That pretty well sums it up for you, doesn't it? You're not designed for meandering conversations that have endless rabbit trails. They aren't a part of your makeup, and you don't want them to be a part of your marriage unless you have intentionally prepared your mind and carved out your time to have one.

> Control is a hard-edged word; it has — at least it seems to have — no poetry in it.
>
> *Judith Viorst*

Nope, your goal in a conversation is to gather the essential information you need and to convey information that you believe your spouse needs to know. That's it. Enough said.

Too blunt? Well, that's how your spouse sometimes feels. Your communication can have a sharp point to it, whether you mean it or not. You can also be an impatient listener. In other words, you probably figure out what your

spouse is trying to say long before your spouse has fin-
ished, and you are ready to fix his or her perception as
soon as given the chance.

Your Approach to Conflict

When your spouse disagrees with you, it only fortifies
your determination to win. "My wife will take a stand and
stick to it no matter
what," a newly mar-
ried husband told
us. "She becomes
so convinced she's
right that she
doesn't spend any energy trying to see my side. I feel like
I'm married to an attorney." That's life with a Take-Charge
Spouse. It's not that you don't want to find a solution, you
just want—ideally—for your spouse first to acknowledge
that you are right. Then you're ready to find a solution,
and quickly.

> We will either find a way or
> make one.
>
> *Hannibal, Carthaginian General*

In fact, you don't like to let conflict linger. You want to
get it out on the table and find a resolution. Of course,
that's not always easy in a relationship that requires compromise. As a person who doesn't struggle with self-confidence, humility is one of your biggest hurdles. Add to
that your predilection toward anger and you're bound to
have some intense marital conflicts.

Your Approach to Sex and Intimacy

Because you're a no-nonsense person, you are likely
to be upfront with your sexual needs in your marriage.
That is, you're likely to initiate sex whenever you desire.
You're not necessarily inclined to draw it out, either.
The proverbial "quickie" was designed with you in mind
(especially if you are the husband). Sure, you enjoy those
romantic encounters with your spouse when time is of

no concern, but you also mean business. You're likely to make it clear to your spouse exactly what you like and what you don't.

Of all the four Love Styles, yours is the one that is most likely to use sex as tension relief. You sometimes view sex as something you need to do to get your life back in balance (to continue being productive). On occasion, "intimate moments" in your marriage are more about relieving stress than building connection.

Your Approach to Finances

You love a challenge—especially a financial challenge. Sure it may cause you anxiety, but this domain of marriage is tangible and measurable. As a person who loves control, it's right in your sweet spot. You can set a goal, devise a plan, and execute it like nobody's business. This means you're likely to have a goal for savings, a goal for spending—and a goal for your spouse. That's right. You tend to see yourself as the banker in the relationship, determining how much your spouse should spend.

This does not necessarily mean that you balance the books and pay the bills. You may be content to delegate that to your spouse. But you're sure to monitor the process with a watchful eye. And when your spouse's spending crosses the line, you have no trouble pointing that out. After all, you have a financial goal to reach and a plan to maintain.

Your Approach to Free Time

This is a tough one for you. Why? Because you don't have "free" time. You don't have a minute to spare. You're back-to-back and double-booked. You are so busy being productive that you often find it excruciatingly difficult to simply do nothing. And so you fall into two patterns that are equally disconcerting for most spouses.

First, you tend to overamp on structuring your free time by planning out each minute. Even what appears to be "relaxation" for you is likely to serve a productive purpose. A party is an opportunity to network, for example. Or while sitting by the pool on vacation with your spouse, you spend your time working or talking on your cell phone or using your BlackBerry—completely contaminating an opportunity to connect with your spouse. You're likely to enjoy competitive sports, highly interactive hobbies, and taking naps at concerts. You can go through an art museum in record time—and be the "expert" on what was good and what was not at the other end!

> It's a little like wrestling a gorilla. You don't quit when you're tired. You quit when the gorilla is tired.
>
> *Robert Strauss*

Second, you tend to crash rather than rest. People who run fast eventually need a time to recuperate. So just as you live hard, you also "rest" hard, retreating like a grumpy grizzly bear to your cave where you don't want to be bothered.

How You Can Better Love Your Spouse

As a person who likes to be in control—a person who is focused on productivity and speed—there are several specific actions you can take that are sure to improve your marriage. We dedicate the closing section of this chapter to highlighting these actions and wishing you the very best in becoming a better spouse.

Devise Some Marital Reminders

Whenever a business needs you to renew your contract or pay your bill, they send you a reminder letter. It's typically a gentle nudge to get you to take action. Well, as a person on the go, that's exactly what you need in your marriage. You need some mechanisms built into your life to remind you that you're married. Because you are task-driven, you sometimes become so focused on a professional project that you take your eyes off your personal project, your marriage.

I (Les) am the first to confess that I'm a Take-Charge Spouse. Some years ago I thought I could check a bunch of "loving behaviors" off my to-do list with Leslie by using a nifty feature on our voicemail system. It's called "future delivery." It allows you to record a message now and then determine the day you want it to be delivered in the future. I decided to record a dozen or so loving messages to Leslie and then program each to be sent on various days in the coming month. Boom! I could check that issue off my list for a while.

At first, Leslie was pleased to receive them. "Hey, thanks for that nice message today," she'd say. "What message?" I'd ask, before remembering what I had done days earlier. A few messages into this, Leslie began to catch on to what I had done. Suddenly, the messages weren't so meaningful. Truth be told, they weren't coming from the heart. I was trying to take a shortcut, and it left both of us unsatisfied.

In reality, like you, I simply needed some reminders to focus my attention on my spouse. I needed a prompt to be sure I was sincerely tuned into my marriage—rather than being consumed by an upcoming book deadline, a university project, or a speaking engagement. So, I began to send myself a few "future delivery" reminders, this time via my own electronic calendar. At times that I designate, I plug in reminders for various things I want to convey to Leslie or do with her. These might be reminders to ask her how I can help her this week, wash her car and fill it with gas, take her to dinner, take the kids out and give her a quiet evening at home. You get the idea. I simply place reminders on my calendar that increase the odds of my investing in our marriage.

As a task-oriented person yourself, I'm sure you see the value in doing this.

Cultivate Patience

Every spouse needs to get a lock on patience, but this quality seems to be especially challenging for the Take-Charge Spouse. Relative to the other three Love Styles, you have a low tolerance for frustration. And if you boil patience down to its essence, it is the loving response to frustration. Think about it. Frustration tests our capacity to be patient. Have you ever watched a small child trying to thread a needle? You see the child, again and again, trying to push the blunt and frazzled end of the thread through the eye of an unsteady needle. Do you wait through two attempts, four attempts, or six attempts before snatching it away and doing it yourself?

Since you live your life with urgency, your threshold for tolerating frustration can be exceedingly low. Yet you cannot be a truly loving spouse without a healthy dose of patience. In the apostle Paul's famous love poem of 1 Corinthians 13, he begins his litany of loving qualities with this one—patience. In the classic King James Version, it says, "Charity suffereth long" (v. 4). Patience is measured by our ability to endure something we'd rather not. For you, especially, love is patient. Love "suffereth long" whenever you give up your compulsion to be in control. Love is patient in your life whenever you surrender your desire to grab the reins from your spouse.

Love is patient in your life whenever you calmly endure difficulty or inconvenience in your marriage without complaint. And love is patient in your life whenever you stifle a critical comment by biting your tongue.

Okay. We know. This patience thing can be a tough one for you. But if you hone this quality, if you work at it, it will pay off in countless ways in your marriage. As Edmund Burke said, "Our patience will achieve more than our force."

Slow Down

It's in your DNA to move faster than most. You do everything with expediency and efficiency. The only time you slow down is when you decide to. Here, we simply want to remind you to make that decision—for the sake of your spouse.

To help you do just that, we want to give you an unlikely example: the common ant. That's right, those tiny little creatures that never seem to stop working. A recently published study revealed that worker ants sacrifice time and efficiency in order to teach other ants how to find food.[6] When an ant goes out to find food, she will often choose another ant to accompany her. If the second ant doesn't know the way to the food source, the leader will teach her through a process called "tandem running." As the teacher runs along the path to food, the student follows behind and will often stop to locate landmarks. When the student is ready, she will run forward and tap her teacher

> Few things in the world are more powerful than a positive push…A smile. A word of optimism and hope. And knowing you can do it when things are tough."
>
> *Richard M. DeVos*

on her back legs. This process is extremely beneficial for the student. Ants participating in tandem running located a food source in an average of 201 seconds, while ants searching for food on their own took an average of 310 seconds (a 35 percent difference). However, the study found that the lead ants traveled up to four times faster when they were not accompanied by a student.

If the leader didn't want to be slowed down this much, researchers also observed that some would simply carry a follower on their backs and drop them off at the food source. This technique was three times faster than tandem running. But here's the catch: the carried ants were not able to remember how to get back to the food source again.

Learning to slow down goes hand in glove with cultivating patience. As you slow down enough to practice "tandem running" with your spouse, you'll cultivate patience in the process and enjoy a more satisfying and deeper connection with your mate.

Put a Lid on Your Anger

If you haven't learned to do this already, it is essential that you get a grip on your anger. "Anger is a momentary madness," said the ancient Roman poet Horace, "so control your passion or it will control you." We couldn't agree more. We've seen too many good-hearted marriages seriously punctured by the sharp darts of angry words. You can't allow this to happen to you.

What can you do to put a lid on your anger? Allow us to suggest two things. First, know that you are not responsible for being angry, only for how you respond to and use anger once it appears. That's why the Bible says, "In your anger do not sin" (Eph. 4:26). Everyone was created with a capacity to experience passionate anger. But for the quick-tempered spouse, anger becomes a self-defeating rage.

Second, you can curb anger by knowing what is likely to trigger it for you. Chances are, you are most likely to have a quick temper when you are fatigued, belittled, frustrated, or rejected. Identifying exactly which one of these is making you angry in the moment will go a long way to helping you manage it.

And third, don't make your spouse a *scapegoat*. The term comes from the Old Testament reference to an innocent goat who carried the sins of the people and was sent into the desert to die.[7] You see, you're most likely to reveal your anger to the person who loves you the most. Why? Because that's where you feel safest. You may actually be upset at your boss or your child or your pastor, for example, but you end up lashing out at your spouse because he or she is safer to get mad at. Refuse to make your spouse a scapegoat.

Lean Into Grace

On June 11, 2002, one of the most popular shows on American television made its debut. *American Idol* set out to discover the best singers in the country though a series of nationwide auditions. The format unveiled a panel of judges who quickly became famous for their particular styles of critiquing the contestants: Paula Abdul, gracious but not always truthful; Simon Cowell with the aggressive approach, truthful but rarely gracious; and Randy Jackson, truthful and usually gracious at the same time.

You could take a lesson from Randy. Because, if truth be told, you probably lean closer than you think to Simon Cowell's aggressive style in your own marriage. But when you combine your natural bluntness with grace, it tempers your brusqueness and softens your candor. It's what enables you to "[speak] the truth in love."[8]

Truth without grace is judgment. In marriage, it says hurtful things like: "You're kidding me! I specifically asked you to leave the door unlocked. Because of you, I've been waiting here, locked out, all this time. How dumb can you be?" Grace, on the other hand, says: "I know it was an unusual request, and you locked it out of habit. I could have done the same thing. Don't worry about it."

> Grace isn't a little prayer you chant before receiving a meal. It's a way to live.
>
> *Jackie Windspear*

Grace comes from the Greek word *charis*. It means *gift*. It's not earned. It's not deserved. That's what makes grace so valuable in marriage. In fact, it just may be the most valuable gift you ever give your spouse.

Where to Go from Here

Well, there you have it, a summary of your personal Love Style as the Take-Charge Spouse. Of course, you're likely to have a secondary Love Style as indicated on your report from the online L.O.V.E. Style Assessment. So feel free to move next to the chapter describing that Love Style.

If your spouse has completed the online L.O.V.E. Style Assessment, we also suggest you turn to the chapter that summarizes his or her style(s). Even though it is written to your spouse, it will help you gain a deeper understanding of your partner.

You may find it interesting to read the other chapters in this section of the book as well. Even if they don't apply directly to your own Love Style, they can sometimes serve as a helpful way of contrasting your style to the others.

Once you are ready, you'll want to move to Part Three of the book, where you'll learn how you can put your specific Love Styles to work for you.

For Reflection and Discussion

1. How well does this chapter describe you? Give it a percentage ranking and explain why. Be specific. In other words, back up your ranking with a few specific examples.

2. As you consider how you are hardwired for love, what is one specific thing that your spouse could do to better love you? Why might it be difficult for him or her to do this?

3. When it comes to how you can better love your spouse, which item in this chapter is something you can immediately put into practice and how? Also, which item will be most challenging for you and why?

WORKBOOK EXERCISE
for the Take-Charge Spouse

If you're using the optional his/her interactive workbooks, you'll want to turn to the exercise designed specifically for you to apply this chapter to your marriage. It contains several brief exercises that are sure to make this information come alive in your relationship.

OPTIMIST: THE ENCOURAGING SPOUSE

Love is an act of faith, and whoever is of little faith
is also of little love.

Erich Fromm

WITH AN OPTIMIST Love Style, you are People-Oriented
and Fast-Paced. The combination of these two dispositions makes you an Encouraging Spouse. Note where you
land in the four Love Style quadrants:

We'll begin this chapter by exploring your deepest
needs. These
are the needs
you must have
met in order to
function at your
optimal level—
especially in
your marriage.
Speaking of
your optimal
level, we'll move
from there to
"You at Your
Best," looking

	Project-Oriented	People-Oriented
Fast-Paced	Leader The Take-Charge Spouse	**Optimist** The Encouraging Spouse
Slow-Paced	Evaluator The Careful Spouse	Validator The Devoted Spouse

at the five traits that emerge from within you when you are doing well and are operating in your groove. Of course, we will also take a look at "You at Your Worst." We'll look at the five traits that come into view when your deeper needs are not being met.

Next, we'll turn to "How You're Hardwired for Love." In other words, we'll explore how your unique combination of personality traits blend together to create who you are as a spouse and what you are looking for in your relationship.

> A pessimist sees the difficulty in every opportunity; an optimist sees the opportunity in every difficulty.
>
> *Winston Churchill*

This will take us to how you function within "The Five Domains of Real-Life Marriage." These include communication, conflict, sex, finances, and free time. We'll take a close look at how you approach each one.

Finally, we'll give you some practical ways to "Better Love Your Spouse." After you understand your own deep needs and how they shape your approach to marriage, you are poised to become much better at loving your partner at a deeper level.

Before we jump in, we want you to keep in mind that you will likely read something here or there that you don't agree with. In other words, you might think that a particular trait we're exploring doesn't come close to describing you. That's okay. Don't let that interfere with the content you find helpful. Assuming you've taken the online L.O.V.E. Style Assessment, you already know that your personality is too complex to fit neatly into one box. In all likelihood, you are a combination of Love Styles where one is more dominant than the other. That being the case, we don't expect every description in this chapter to fit you perfectly.

Now, take a deep breath. Keep an open mind. Tune in to what rings true to your experience and set aside what doesn't. And take your time as you discover your own Love Style.

Your Deepest Needs

As an Encouraging Spouse, you crave approval. It's in your DNA. You feed off of winning the acceptance of those around you—especially your spouse. You thrive on compliments. You have a built-in radar detector for approval that never turns off. You constantly monitor your approval rating, looking for the slightest movement in either the positive or negative direction. If it goes down, you immediately shift tactics to gain more favor. If you sense your spouse doesn't like what you're wearing, even slightly, for example, you feel compelled to try on something different.

In addition to approval, you want affection. That means you want your spouse to consider your desires and take special care to meet them. But even if your spouse doesn't shower you with affection, you're likely to be affectionate yourself. In other words, you do everything you can to enjoy a deep and affectionate friendship that involves warm and inspiring conversations. It's one of your deepest needs.

> A pessimist only sees the dark side of the clouds, and mopes; a philosopher sees both sides and shrugs; an optimist doesn't see the clouds at all—he's walking on them.
>
> *Leonard L. Levinson*

You also have a deep need for fun. Of course, everyone likes to have fun. But you make sure there's fun to be had. You don't just go to a party, you *are* a party. Your outgoing and cheerful personality makes you popular and draws people to you. You like to joke, laugh, and entertain. For you, fun is nearly anything that's spontaneous, surprising, adventurous, unrestricted, and unplanned. And if something is not fun, you either make it fun or you lose interest.

> To love what you do and feel that it matters—how could anything be more fun?
>
> *Katharine Graham*

As a person with an Optimist Love Style, you are on the hunt for attention, affection, approval, and acceptance—all while having a good time.

**The Encouraging Spouse's Motto:
If it's worth doing—make it fun.**

You at Your Best

Bob Basso, a corporate team builder, said, "If it's not fun, you're not doing it right." Surely you agree—whatever the activity. And plenty of other people agree that you're doing plenty of things right. Here are some of the qualities you display when you're at your best.

Fun-loving

We've already noted that you *need* to have fun, that having a good time is hardwired into your being. But you're also great at creating a fun time for others. Your fun is contagious. You enliven conversations—not to mention your marriage—with laughter and playfulness. You lighten the mood with your spontaneous high spirits. You have the amazing gift of making people feel better.

Positive

"When you get into a tight place and everything goes against you, till it seems as though you could not hold on a minute longer," said abolitionist Harriet Beecher Stowe, "never give up then, for that is just the place and time that the tide will turn." She's preaching to the choir when it comes to you.

Why? Because more than any of the other Love Styles, you embody a positive and optimistic spirit. You know something good is just about to happen. You're banking on it. Your upbeat attitude is one of the greatest assets you bring to your marriage.

Persuasive

You have a winsome way that can be very influential. It's a leadership quality that makes you able to sway opinions. You're convincing and believable. People are interested in your opinions (and you're rarely shy about giving them) because your thoughts matter to others. Of course, your persuasiveness is not lost on your spouse. You have tremendous influence, whether it's recognized or not, in your marriage. You may take a soft-sell or a hard-sell approach. Either way, you're very persuasive.

Sociable

When people think of you, they often use the word "warm." It's a way of saying they like you, that you are pleasant, kind, welcoming, and friendly. You warm other people's hearts.

You probably take this trait for granted, but it's fre-

> So long as we are loved by others I should say that we are almost indispensible.
>
> *Robert Louis Stevenson*

quently in short supply. Thus the Japanese proverb: "One kind word can warm three winter months." Kindness is rare—except when you're around. It's a quality that drew your spouse to you from the beginning.

Encouraging

You literally fill other people, especially your spouse, with courage and confidence. Your natural energy and optimism infuse your relationships with assurance. You express your belief in people you care about. And you don't shy away from spurring them on to whatever it is they aspire to. You're their publicist, promoter, and cheerleader combined. And because you also bring the power of persuasiveness into the picture, you inspire like few others.

You at Your Worst

"The basis of optimism," said Oscar Wilde, "is sheer terror." Whether you agree with that sentiment or not, we can tell you that the scary side of your personality emerges when your deeper needs aren't getting met. That's when your optimistic outlook turns dark. When you are at your worst, you tend to demonstrate the following traits:

Conflict Avoidant

You don't like to rock the proverbial boat. On the surface, this sounds admirable. But it creates an uneasiness and lack of genuineness in your relationships. Because you tend to bury your anger and sweep difficulties under the rug, you give up authenticity. For example, you'll say something that's not altogether true in order to keep your spouse from getting mad. You go along just to keep the peace. You'll do what's most peaceful instead of what's right.

> The man who cannot endure to have his errors and shortcomings brought to the surface and made known, but tries to hide them, is unfit to walk the highway of truth.
>
> *James Allen*

A relationship can only take so much of this phoniness before you're found out and a crack emerges in your partner's capacity to trust you.

Dramatic

You can make a lot of fuss about nothing. Sometimes it's for sheer entertainment. This happens when you turn something trivial into a soap opera because it makes for better storytelling. But sometimes it's done for sympathy. You'll make a lot of fuss about nothing when your emotions get the better of you. If you're especially sensitive about being criticized for your mathematic abilities, for example, you can ramp up a dramatic story about how your third grade teacher demoralized you in front of the class when you missed a math problem. That engenders sympathy, even if the story contains only a grain of truth.

Easily Distracted

Your fun-loving ways can make it tough to sit through a task you see as boring. It could be a lecture, a work project, reading directions, or doing some housework. That's when you tend to daydream, joke with colleagues, or take frequent breaks. The result, of course, is that you don't finish the task at hand. This can also occur because you are suddenly struck by a whim. You want a cup of coffee. But not just any coffee. You want that special blend that is only sold across town. Again, your impulsive nature and positive spirit can keep you off-task.

Prone to Procrastinate

This dreaded quality probably comes as no surprise. You put off nearly anything that isn't fun or may represent conflict. Maybe it's been months since you've balanced your checkbook, for example. The thought of doing such a tedious job makes you want to either put it off some more or just switch banks. Your procrastination is often counterproductive and needless—and it almost always results in more stress for you. Still, you can't seem to buck up and do the things you dread. Does it impact your marriage? Of course! You already know it can drive your spouse nuts.

Forgetful

Because you are hard-wired as a people-pleaser and because you were designed for fun, you can easily become forgetful. If your spouse wants you to join a phone call to a family friend right now—even though you're supposed to drop off a package at the post office before it closes—you'll likely forget about the more mundane task of mailing your package.

The point is that you get easily sidetracked. Even if you do have a schedule to maintain, a list of tasks to do, or a financial plan to follow, you can still end up being late, not remembering, and overspending, because you got caught up in something or someone that seemed more fun or meaningful at the moment.

How You're Hardwired to Love

You approach marriage like you approach nearly everything else. With a question: *Are we having fun yet?* Your marriage, ideally, is full of romance and whimsy. You expect passion, enthusiasm, and excitement. Most of all, you expect to feel accepted and loved—deeply loved. In other words, you want an affectionate marriage, free of tension and overflowing with joy.

Relative to others, you don't waste too much time whining or complaining about what your marriage could be or should be. After all, problems and conflict only diminish your fun. And you certainly don't want to have to "work" on your marriage. Sure, you're willing to exert effort to make it the best marriage it can be, but you'll do it by way of having fun and creativity.

Rick, an Encouraging Spouse, has an energetic personality that is always looking on the bright side. So when his marriage was going through a bit of a rough spot, he didn't look up "marriage counselor" in the phone book to schedule an appointment. Instead, he scheduled a vacation. Without notice, he literally whisked his wife off to Europe for nine days without packing a single suitcase. "I wanted it to be a true adventure," he told us. "We didn't have reservations at a hotel, we didn't have an itinerary—and we barely had money. But I knew we could buy what we needed once we got there. We were flying blind," he said with glee. "We had a blast and it got us out of our bickering mode."

That's how a person with an Optimist Love Style approaches a marriage problem. Of course, it's not always that extravagant. You've undoubtedly created some fun in your marriage with a few surprises of your own. And you probably relish the chance to tell the stories (with a bit of embellishment for good measure).

Speaking of telling stories, you need your partner's full attention when you're doing just that. In fact, you need your partner's listening ear whenever you're talking. And you *do* like to talk. You need your spouse to listen carefully, paying special attention to your feelings, as you describe your day or recount a meeting. This is one of your sure signs of being loved. If you're not getting the attention you want, you will either try harder—by making your story more dramatic or emotional—or, if truly hurt, you will shutdown.

As an Optimist Spouse, you express your love with an abundance of affection and encouragement. And you deeply want the same from your spouse. But chances are that you don't always get as much love as you'd like. Because you are designed to seek approval, you don't do well if the affection and encouragement in your marriage is drying up. That's when you're likely to pout, mope, sulk, or withdraw—hoping your spouse picks up on your "clues" and replenishes the affection by showering you with love.

The bottom line is that you are hardwired to love by making your marriage exciting, passionate, affectionate, and fun.

How the Encouraging Spouse Defines Love
Love is...Being fully attentive and giving
each other affection and acceptance.

You and the Five Domains of Real-Life Marriage

Every marriage, regardless of its stage, has specific domains that can become sticking points between a husband and wife. This is especially true for couples who have not explored how their personal Love Styles impact and shape each one of these domains. These include: communication, conflict, sex, finances, and free time.

Here's how you approach each one.

Your Approach to Communication

You're never at a loss for words. You love to talk. You bask in the attention of being listened to. It's one of your most telling ways of monitoring your approval rating with your spouse. The more your spouse listens, the more you feel loved. Like the host of a late night talk show, you're adept at moving the conversation to be as entertaining as possible.

It's not that you don't listen to your spouse talk, by the way. You do. You listen very well. You're a great listener. It's just that you want the listening to go both ways, or it's no fun. More often than not, you prefer to get your message heard first. It helps you to be a better listener.

Communication for you is a primary means for giving and receiving love in your marriage. If you're having communication problems, you are having marriage problems.

Your Approach to Conflict

You abhor conflict. You avoid directly confronting the issue at hand even if your spouse wants to discuss it. You do this by changing the subject, putting off the discussion until later, or simply not bringing it up. You will sometimes bury your own needs or conceal your own desires simply to avoid tension. You'll swallow your feelings and wear a smile to conceal your distress. You'll put up with something you don't like from your spouse for fear addressing it will cause conflict. And when things get rough, you'll withdraw from the relationship altogether by sulking.

Be aware that conflict avoidance is different than conflict prevention. The former is unhealthy and the latter is not. Chances are good that you do both. In addition to avoiding conflict by concealing your true feelings, you also prevent potential conflict in your marriage by knowing what is likely to trigger a heated disagreement with your spouse.

Your Approach to Sex and Intimacy

As a person with an Optimist Love Style, you are likely to be fun, energetic, and creative in the bedroom (as long as you feel rested). While you don't always take the lead (especially if you are the woman), you often set the mood. You're eager to please your spouse. You enjoy the anticipation of lovemaking, and you let your spouse know that you're looking forward to it.

You view sex as a means of giving and receiving love. Just as important as feeling good physically is feeling loved emotionally. If you're feeling put down or rejected in any way by your spouse, you're not about to open up freely in the bedroom. In other words, you don't use sex to make up for words that need to be spoken. You want to express love verbally before and after you make love physically.

Your Approach to Finances

Most people don't equate fun with finances. The mere thought of reading through the documents for a home loan or investment you're considering drains you of your last drop of energy, and you seldom take the time to do so. You have an optimistic outlook when dealing with finances. Therefore, you can also be a little susceptible when it comes to money. You can be gullible on occasion and even irresponsible with money matters.

If you happen to be the spouse in your marriage who is balancing the books, you may have a tendency to be a bit casual about it and can more easily "write off" the small stuff instead of wrestling with the last few pennies. You approach money matters with as much enthusiasm as you can. If something catches your eye and you want to buy it, you'll do a good job of selling your spouse on moving forward. You'll also want to tell your spouse when you have met a financial goal, and you'll expect a bit of celebration. Your greatest financial fear is displeasing your partner and feeling rejected when it comes to money matters.

Your Approach to Free Time

Here we hit your sweet spot. You love "free" time. You thrive on it. When you're rested and your deeper needs are being met, you're ready to make the most of it. You're ready for adventure. You're ready for a new experience. And, by all means, you want to do something with your free time that makes for a good story. You want to do something you can tell your friends about.

Better yet, you like to get out and spend time as a couple with other friends. You like frequent interactions with family and friends. You start to get cabin fever if you're cooped up too long, just the two of you. In the church foyer after the Sunday service, you're likely to hook up with another couple for brunch. If you're going to a game or the movies, you'll invite friends to join you. And, of course, you love a good party.

The point is that you're not one to stay still for long when you have free time. Sure, you can relax or hang out for a time, but if you do, you prefer it be somewhere fun. You want to hit the spa or walk along the beach. Strange as it sounds, you want your relaxing to be an adventure. And you don't need a detailed or structured plan. Yuck! You like discovery and spontaneity.

How You Can Better Love Your Spouse

As a person who likes to win approval—a person who is active and focused on people—there are several specific actions you can take that are sure to improve your marriage. So we dedicate the closing section of this chapter to highlighting these actions and wishing you the very best in becoming a better spouse.

Be Willing to Disagree

You probably don't want to hear this, but you've got to learn how to fight a good fight. Your capacity to go with the flow and conceal your true feelings as a means of maintaining peace in your marriage is not healthy.

It stunts growth and authenticity. Honesty is a cornerstone of marriage. Without authenticity, your relationship eventually becomes hollow. Your love will ultimately feel empty.

To help you be more honest with your spouse, let's remember the reason you sometimes dread it. You too often conceal your true feelings—those you imagine might hurt your spouse—because you fear rejection. If you disagree with your

> *Integrity is telling myself the truth. And honesty is telling the truth to other people.*
>
> *Spencer Johnson*

spouse, you fear your partner will withhold affection and love. That's just not true. Sure, you'll make some temporary waves in your relationship and travel some passing rough seas because of your willingness to disagree, but in doing so you will also build a fortified relationship that weathers life's inevitable storms.

The next time you feel tempted to say, "But I don't want to hurt my spouse's feelings," replace it with, "I'm willing to risk a bit of tension in the present for a stronger and more authentic relationship in the future."

Being sensitive and responsive to your partner's needs is a valuable quality. It's certainly admirable to minimize conflict—but not at the price of being phony. You can love your spouse better by being more authentic when you have a differing desire, opinion, or feeling than he or she does.

Shoot Straight

This one goes along with being honest. You see, as a person who craves love and acceptance, you will sometimes hide your shortcomings, mistakes, and blunders. Jennifer is married to a penny-pinching spouse who likes an accounting of their finances. Whenever Jennifer comes home from nearly any kind of shopping, her husband asks how much things cost.

"You went to that gourmet grocery? How much were these tomatoes?" he'll prod.

"I think they were on sale," Jennifer replies, while craftily avoiding an answer. "Aren't they gorgeous?"

Knowing his wife's predilection to hide the truth in moments like these, he quickly combs through the grocery bags to find the receipt. "You paid almost ten dollars for a pound of tomatoes!" he exclaims.

While the price may be disconcerting, it's the fact that Jennifer didn't shoot straight with him about how much she spent that really irritates him. These little deceptions diminish his trust in her.

The same is true in your marriage, and it involves far more than just money. You love your spouse better when you shoot straight about everything. Especially when you are at fault. "One of the hardest things in this world is to admit you are wrong," said Benjamin Disraeli. "And nothing is more helpful in resolving a situation than its frank admission." So true. Don't be afraid of 'fessing up to your foibles. While you think it will drive your spouse away, it will actually bring you closer because you're becoming more trustworthy.

Moderate Your Verbiage

It's not that you necessarily feel the need to fill every waking moment with the sound of your own voice. But you, more than most, have a tendency to take a simple question like, "How was your day?" or "What happened at the meeting?" and answer it with every detail.

Some people talk too much because they feel insecure or because they like the sound of their own voice. Some talk too much because they are opinionated or because they are self-absorbed. In all likelihood, these are not the reasons that propel you to talk at length. You risk talking too much because you long for acceptance and approval.

Henry, a classic Encouraging Spouse, worked in retail sales. In fact, he excelled at his job, and he loved the personal interactions with his customers. His wife, on the other hand, was an Evaluator Spouse and worked as a librarian. She liked a little time to unwind and put her mind in neutral at the end of the workday. Not Henry. He could go on and on about the interesting customers he met and the changes on the showroom floor. He loved to describe all the details. His wife? Not so much. In fact, in an effort to have Henry moderate his verbiage, she would pick up the newspaper or a magazine and avoid eye contact. No matter. Henry would keep talking for a bit more. Then, realizing his wife was no longer interested, he'd feel rejected and clam up.

In time, Henry learned to moderate his excessive talking by not taking his wife's signals personally. That's the key. He realized that she was not wired for conversations the same way he was. Too much talking wore her out. In fact, as he was learning to curb his conversations, he had a phrase that helped him: "Information Overload." When he picked up on one of her clues, like a lack of eye contact, he would say those two words in the form of a question. That self-awareness created an opportunity for his wife to say keep going or ask him to wind it up. Either way, it helped him learn not to take it personally and to moderate his verbiage.

You can do the same thing for your spouse. It may seem strange to you, because from your perspective talking is a means to becoming closer, but for your spouse, it may be too much of a good thing. All you have to do is ask.

Respect the Plan

Let's be honest, you're not a person with a plan. You don't crave structure or routine. Why live the same day twice, right? You're more apt to shoot from the hip, make snap decisions, and improvise. Sure, you have goals and you accomplish things, but not necessarily because you thrive on organization and strict schedules.

Your spouse, on the other hand, just might. For example, if you are married to a Leader or an Evaluator, your spouse hardly does anything without a purpose and a plan. If you want to love your spouse better, you're going to need to respect your spouse's plans.

No doubt you're fine with something as simple as going out on the town for a date night with no plans of where to eat or what to do. Stumbling onto a new restaurant, good or bad, is part of the adventure. But your spouse may have other plans, literally. Your partner may want to go online and read the reviews of a movie or call ahead for a dinner reservation. In other words, he or she wants a plan. When you respect that plan, your spouse feels loved.

> It pays to plan ahead. It wasn't raining when Noah built the ark.
>
> *Anonymous*

By the way, you also love your spouse when you bring your good-natured spontaneity into the relationship. You add great value to the marriage with this trait. You do that automatically. We're simply reminding you here that it goes both ways. Your spouse's planning and structure also add value to your marriage. The more you see that and respect it, the better you love your spouse.

Thomas Edison said, "Good fortune happens when opportunity meets good planning." You'll be saying the same thing once you give your spouse's plans some merit.

Finish What You Start

William James said, "Nothing is so fatiguing as the eternal hanging on of an uncompleted task." Know the feeling? Everyone has uncompleted tasks that nag at them on occasion. We all procrastinate from time to time because of indecision, lack of time, lack of priority, or plain old fear. But you, more than most, tend to start projects with a gust of excitement and enthusiasm, then end up putting them on hold, not necessarily because of a lack of priority or fear, but because they're no longer as fun as they were at the start. Or because something more fun came along. Or because your optimism caused you to underestimate the amount of time it would take to complete them. Whatever your reasons, your lack of follow-through can be detrimental to your marriage.

> Optimism doesn't wait on facts.
> It deals with prospects.
>
> *Norman Cousins*

For starters, it can cause anxiety for your spouse (especially if your partner is either a Leader or an Evaluator). Bubbly Brittany, with a true Optimist Love Style, doesn't mind last-minute chaos, frenzied thinking, and messy situations. Since it's more fun to hurry on to the finish, she doesn't mind cutting corners or hiding messes in cabinets, closets, and drawers.

This kind of disorganization drives her spouse crazy. He likes order. He likes predictability and plans. He likes follow-through that doesn't sacrifice quality. So you can imagine how he feels when he opens up the drawer in the kitchen where he expects to find scissors and they're nowhere to be seen. Brittany needed them, it turns out, to individually wrap in cellophane twenty-five miniature tractors filled with candy corn for her son's third-grade class party. She got through about half of them when she remembered that wet towels have been sitting in her washer since yesterday. She rushed to restart the wash and, later, couldn't find the scissors (which are now in the laundry room) to finish the tractor-wrapping project that's spread over the dining room table.

You get the idea. You've lived it. You know the fatigue that can set into your marriage when it's enveloped by unfinished tasks. That's why you can better love your spouse by finishing what you start and staying on task as best you can.

Where to Go from Here

There you have it, a summary of your personal Love Style as the Encouraging Spouse. Of course, you're likely to have a secondary Love Style as indicated on your report from the online L.O.V.E. Style Assessment. So feel free to move next to the chapter describing that style.

If your spouse has completed the online L.O.V.E. Style Assessment, we also suggest you turn to the chapter that summarizes his or her style(s). Even though it is written to your spouse, it will help you gain a deeper understanding of your partner.

Of course, you may find it interesting to read the other chapters in this section of the book as well. Even if they don't apply directly to your own Love Style, they can sometimes serve as a helpful way of contrasting your style to the others.

Once you are ready, you'll want to eventually move to Part Three of the book, where you'll learn how you can put your specific Love Styles to work for you.

For Reflection and Discussion

1. How well does this chapter describe you? Give it a percentage ranking and explain why. Be specific. In other words, back up your ranking with a few specific examples.

2. As you consider how you are hardwired for love, what is one specific thing that your spouse could do to better love you? Why might it be difficult for your partner to do this?

3. When it comes to ways you can better love your spouse, which item in this chapter is something you can immediately put into practice and how? Also, which item will be most challenging for you and why?

 # WORKBOOK EXERCISE
for the Encouraging Spouse

If you're electing to use the optional his/her interactive workbooks, you'll want to turn to the exercise designed specifically for you to apply this chapter to your marriage. It contains several brief exercises that are sure to make this information come alive in your relationship.

VALIDATOR: THE DEVOTED SPOUSE

Whatever I have devoted myself to, I have devoted myself completely; in great aims and in small I have always thoroughly been in earnest.

Charles Dickens

WITH A VALIDATOR Love Style, you are People-Oriented and Slow-Paced. The combination of these two dispositions makes you a Devoted Spouse. Note where you land in the four Love Style quadrants:

We'll begin this chapter by exploring your deepest needs. These are the needs you must have met in order to function at your optimal level — especially in

	Project-Oriented	People-Oriented
Fast-Paced	Leader The Take-Charge Spouse	Optimist The Encouraging Spouse
Slow-Paced	Evaluator The Careful Spouse	**Validator** The Devoted Spouse

your marriage. Speaking of your optimal level, we'll move from there to "You at Your Best," looking at the five traits that emerge from within you when you are doing well and are operating in your groove. Of course, we will also take a look at "You at Your Worst." We'll look at the five traits that come into view when your deeper needs are not being met.

Next, we'll turn to "How You're Hardwired for Love." In other words, we'll explore how your unique combination of personality traits blends together to create who you are as a spouse and what you are looking for in your relationship.

This will take us to how you function within "The Five Domains of Real-Life Marriage." These include communication, conflict, sex, finances, and free time. We'll take a close look at how you approach each one.

Finally, we'll give you some practical ways to "Better Love Your Spouse." After you understand your own deep needs and how they shape your approach to marriage, you are poised to become much better at loving your partner at a deeper level.

Before we jump in, we want you to keep in mind that you will likely read something here or there that you don't agree with. In other words, you might think that a particular trait we're exploring doesn't come close to describing you. That's okay. Don't let that interfere with the content you find helpful. Assuming you've taken the online L.O.V.E. Style Assessment, you already know that your personality is too complex to fit neatly into one box. In all likelihood, you are a combination of Love Styles where one is more dominant than the other. That being the case, we don't expect every description in this chapter to fit you perfectly.

Now, take a deep breath. Keep an open mind. Tune in to what rings true to your experience and set aside what doesn't. And take your time as you discover your own Love Style.

Your Deepest Needs

As a Devoted Spouse, you require far more harmony and peace than any of the other Love Styles. In fact, having a peaceful home tops your list of needs. You are designed for loyalty, union, and agreement. This means you abhor confrontation and conflict, so much so that you will quietly swallow your own painful feelings to avoid a potential quarrel.

Of course, this repression of frustration can evolve into resentment, but you'll still remain relatively quiet about your discordant feelings to maintain the peace. The only place your true feelings of resentment seem to seep out is when you withdraw even more intensely than you usually do. This leaves your spouse wondering whether or not you are investing in the relationship. Whatever your tactics, your deep need is to keep the peace and maintain harmony.

> Harmony is pure love.
> *Lope de Vega*

You also have a deep need for stability. You like things to be consistent and steady. You love loyalty. You don't want to rock the boat or make waves—and you don't like your spouse to, either. In fact, you're not too keen on change of any kind, unless there's a very good reason and it doesn't negatively impact your relationship. You prefer predictability, not spontaneity. You'll take reliability over exhilarating any day. Larry McMurtry, known for his book *Lonesome Dove*, recalls that his father seldom left his east Texas dirt farm. Comparing his own travels to his father's predictable life, McMurtry admits, "I have looked at many places quickly. My father looked at one place deeply." You're similar to McMurtry's father. You have a deep need for stability.

Because of your Validator Love Style, you not only like to esteem your partner, but also you want to be esteemed and respected by your partner. You may not speak much, but when you do you want your opinions acknowledged, respected, and heard. Regardless of whether or not your spouse actually agrees with what you are saying, you need to be treated with genuine respect. You need your partner to acknowledge that what you are saying is a legitimate expression of your feelings. In other words, you won't stand for being marginalized or dismissed.

> One's action ought to come out of an achieved stillness: not to be mere rushing on.
>
> *D.H. Lawrence*

The Devoted Spouse's Motto:
If it's worth doing—we'll do it together.

You at Your Best

Everyone prizes devotion. And every marriage requires it. But you have a special lock on it. You're literally hardwired for deep devotion in your marriage, and when your needs are being met, your devotion is characterized by several admirable traits. Here are some of them.

Loyal

As a Devoted Spouse, you embody reliability, faithfulness, allegiance, dependability, and perseverance. All of these words are wrapped up in your personality. It goes against your grain to be erratic, unpredictable, or unreliable. It's just not you.

You'll do whatever it takes to follow through and maintain a promise. Your partner can count on you—through good times and bad. You're a rock. You're as loyal as they come.

> The need for devotion to something outside ourselves is even more profound than the need for companionship. If we are not to go to pieces or wither away, we must have some purpose in life; for no man can live for himself alone.
>
> *Ross Parmenter*

Agreeable

Your Validator Love Style brings a delightful agreeableness to the relationship. When you're at your best, this makes you enjoyable, adaptable, and flexible. In other words, you are easy to get along with—even if you might be slow to warm up.

Most people describe you as easygoing because you rarely get upset. And most people, including your spouse, appreciate the fact that you rarely get ruffled.

Thoughtful

You are often attentive, meaning that you are conscientious and considerate. You consider other people's needs. You're kind and caring. While others intend to be more kind and have to work at it, you seem to come by it naturally. What a gift! As the saying goes, "The smallest act of kindness is

> Blessed are the peacemakers: for they shall be called the children of God.
>
> *Matthew 5:9 KJV*

worth more than the grandest intention." When you're at your best, you can put yourself in your partner's shoes more readily than other people. This goes a long way in helping your spouse feel loved and understood.

Tolerant

More than any other Love Style, you personify an extraordinary level of tolerance for those little things that drive other spouses crazy. You seem to be able to look past the "mosquitoes of marriage." In other words, you put up with quirky habits, like chomping ice or leaving dirty socks on the floor.

> Peace is the only battle worth waging.
>
> *Albert Camus*

You endure snoring and room temperatures that aren't to your liking. Of course, you have your limits. Every Devoted Spouse does. But you, more than most, are a very tolerant person.

Nurturing

You are reserved, you don't say as much as others, but you enjoy being around people. And when you are, you're a world-class nurturer. You make others feel cared for and looked after—including your spouse. You literally nourish your partner's soul. You bring out the best in your partner. You probably nourish your partner's physical needs as well. Your spouse is likely never to go hungry when you're around. You nurse physical wounds and illness pretty well, too. You are a caregiver.

You at Your Worst

It's true what they say, that our greatest strengths can have a dark side. So let's take a look at yours. When you are at your worst—when your primary needs aren't getting met—you tend to demonstrate the following traits:

Withdrawn

The more uneasy you feel in a situation, the more withdrawn you get. That is, when your deep needs are not being met, you clam up. You don't divulge your opinions. You may be listening, but you're not offering input. You're not offering any clues as to what's going on inside you.

In control, restrained, and unaffected is how you are perceived in these moments. You become indifferent and unmoved, not revealing anything about what you're feeling. This can be interpreted as unmotivated or passive by your spouse. In these times, you come across as more of an observer than a participant in your own marriage.

> Peace cannot be kept by force. It can only be achieved by understanding.
>
> *Albert Einstein*

Indecisive

You may not see this in yourself, but you can come across as indecisive when you're at your worst. Here's why: Even after you make a decision, you are often slow to talk about it. You may talk around it a bit. Or you may simply hold it inside. But you don't come out boldly with an articulated decision. You fear that your decision may negatively impact your relationship somehow. That's why you keep it inside. Your cautious nature about maintaining peace can cause you to tiptoe around your decisions. That's what makes you come across as ambiguous and hesitant, maybe even wavering and uncertain—even when you're not.

Resistant to Change

Your slow pace becomes even slower when you aren't functioning at your best. Your deep need for stability can render you dull and lifeless. You're content for every day to be the same. What you call a routine, others might call a rut.

You can take dreadfully long to respond to a potential change in your life while your partner waits on you. Your resistance almost always stems from your concern about how the change will impact your relationships—especially your marriage. That's why, on occasion, you can even be seen as headstrong, obstinate, and stubborn in the face of potential change. *After all*, you think, *we agreed on a plan, so why change it at this point?* By the way, you can eventually adapt to change as long as you understand how the change impacts your original plan.

> Stillness of person and steadiness of features are signal marks of good breeding.
> *Oliver Wendell Holmes*

Aloof

Because of your tendency toward withdrawal and a stoic demeanor (a tactic for helping you keep the peace), you tend to bring down any expression of enthusiasm or excitement. You don't join in, even though you may actually be supportive. Because you don't show your emotions, you can diminish your spouse's expressions of excitement. You may very well enjoy being around when something exciting happens, but it doesn't always come through on your face or your verbal expressions. Compared to other Love Styles, you don't tend to celebrate as much. If your spouse has an Optimist Love Style, that can be particularly disheartening for your partner.

Unable to Say No

Because you work so hard to maintain peace in your relationships, you frequently agree to things when your plate is already full and overflowing. This stems partly from your sympathetic nature and the resulting guilt of turning down something that will make another person happy. And it stems partly from your fear of risking a potential rift. You feel like a failure when you can't deliver, yet you struggle to say no because it could jeopardize your relationship. You never, ever want to drop the proverbial ball, but you agree to yet another request that you may not realistically be able to fulfill. It's that internal struggle that makes it tough for you to say no.

How You're Hardwired to Love

Calm and peaceful. That's your approach to marriage. Like everything else in your life, you don't want your marriage to suffer tense moments or edgy exchanges. You're not particularly fond of emotional highs or exuberant expressions. As a person with a Validator Love Style, you're content with a peaceful and agreeable relationship that you can count on. That's it. You prize dependability. Passion and excitement? Not so much. Happiness and joy? Sure, but only if they are a follow-up to the primary pursuits of peace and patience.

Relative to other Love Styles, you sometimes appear to have little energy, and that can impact your marriage. Your partner, for example, may perceive you as not wanting to "work" on your marriage. In fact, relative to other styles, you're pretty good with the status quo. But the very fact that you're reading these words indicates that the perception of you not being motivated to improve your relationship is a false one.

> Some people prefer the certainty of misery to the misery of uncertainty.
>
> *Virginia Satir*

Becky, a nonassertive, Devoted Spouse, loves her husband. She's never wavered in her love for him, but you wouldn't exactly say that she lavishes her husband with warm affection. She's not dreaming of romantic getaways for the two of them. She's not snapping into action with a spontaneous whirlwind of activity to please him. And she's not surprising him with a sexy new negligee, either. Becky expresses her love by being deferential, easygoing, and courteous. Even if she disagrees with her husband, she never raises her voice.

That's the way of the Devoted Spouse. You cultivate harmony and maintain stability in your marriage. You express your love with an abundance of dedication, loyalty, and devotion. Your agreeable spirit, matched with consistency and reliability, are a huge support to your spouse.

By the way, you want your spouse to be and do the same for you. You want your spouse to respect your contribution, even if it isn't loud or flashy. You want to be a team player. You want your spouse to love you by boosting your self-worth, respecting your routines, avoiding conflict and pressure, asking for your input, and including you in conversations even when you're not especially talkative. In short, you give and receive love best through the language of devotion.

How the Devoted Spouse Defines Love
Love is . . . Being reassured that we are
on the same team and working together.

You and the Five Domains of Real-Life Marriage

Every marriage, regardless of its stage, has specific domains that can become sticking points between a husband and wife. This is especially true for couples who have not explored how their personal Love Styles impact and shape each one of these domains. These include: communication, conflict, sex, finances, and free time.

Here's how you approach each one.

Your Approach to Communication

You're typically on the quiet side, keeping many of your feelings carefully hidden from view. You have no need to tell drawn-out and dramatic stories, nor are you compelled to rush a conversation to its point. You don't divulge details unless you're asked about them. You approach your conversations with a sense of serenity and calm, and your spouse needs to patiently draw you out.

Even if something's urgent or exciting, you express it evenly, without heightened emotions. You tend to speak slowly and deliberately.

Your Approach to Conflict

Since peace is just about your highest priority in marriage, you don't experience many external quarrels with your spouse. You keep your conflicts covered up, internalizing your struggles. You rarely, if ever, have an emotional outburst of any kind, and certainly not one of anger. Other Love Styles may air their grievances and stir up tension, but not you. Conflict, for you, is to be avoided at all costs. That may mean burying any unpleasantness that is sure to bring about dissension. It may mean avoiding a particular topic that is bound to cause turmoil. Whatever it takes is fine with you—as long as it maintains the peace.

> That is the happiest conversation where there is no competition, no vanity, but a calm, quiet interchange of sentiments.
>
> *Samuel Johnson*

Your Approach to Sex and Intimacy

You probably shy away from the term *sex*. You're more comfortable with the term "lovemaking." Why? Because it's not about a single, passionate act for you. It's about an expression of relational connection. Foreplay for you is not something that's focused only in the bedroom. It's an ongoing relational tone that sets the stage for eventual passionate play. Also, you don't have a strong need for variety or spontaneity here. Your tendency to be an observer rather than a participant can impact your lovemaking by keeping you from fully "letting go" when you don't feel emotionally safe with your partner. You want your partner to be happy, and you're devoted to a good sex life for that reason as much as any.

Your Approach to Finances

Whether you are adept at financial management or not, you like to have a financial plan. And you want to stick to that plan. It guides your financial decisions. You're likely inclined to be on the thrifty side, but not always. If you are a "saver," you buy into the long-term strategy and you abide by it. If you are a "spender," you like to know what's going on. Whether you are the one to actually balance the books

> Any change, even a change for better, is always accompanied by drawbacks and discomforts.
>
> *Arnold Bennett*

or not in your relationship, you want to be informed of what's going on. You want to be involved. Why? Because you don't like surprises. You certainly don't want your spouse to change the original plan unless there are very good reasons that you both agree on.

Your Approach to Free Time

Your desire to avoid surprises applies to your free time, too. Not surprisingly, you like to have a plan for what the two of you will do next weekend, for example. You don't need a regimented schedule, but a plan you can count on nonetheless. Whether it involves a lot of action or a lot of resting (which is probably your preference) is almost secondary to making sure that your spouse follows through on what you both agreed to. In other words, you don't want your free time spoiled by something that wasn't in the plans. If your spouse doesn't follow through on the plan, if he or she tries to sneak in something you didn't expect, you feel a bit betrayed.

How You Can Better Love Your Spouse

As a person who wants peace at any price, there are several specific actions you can take that are sure to improve the health of your marriage. So we dedicate the closing section of this chapter to highlighting these actions and wishing you the very best in becoming a better spouse.

Express Yourself

What a gift this is to your spouse! He or she is dying for you to open up and talk freely about your feelings. Of course, exposing your honest emotions does not come easily to you. So how can you express yourself more freely? How can you open up and be more vulnerable? It begins by recognizing what's holding you back—your fear of jeopardizing the relationship.

For example, if you're feeling discontent or frustrated by your current job, you don't want to express these sentiments too strongly because you fear it may cause your spouse to worry that your employment may not be stable. So you keep it inside. You fret over the possible squabbling your relationship will suffer because of this disclosure. But did you realize the message that often comes through to your spouse when you do this? Your partner feels like you don't believe he or she is strong enough to handle your feelings. Your spouse feels like you don't have the confidence in the strength of your relationship to explore this terri-

> In family life, love is the oil that eases friction, the cement that binds us closer together, and the music that brings harmony.
>
> *Eva Burrows*

tory. Of course, you don't mean to convey this message, but that's how it often comes through.

If you want to better love your spouse, why not ease into a bit of vulnerability by expressing some feelings? You can initiate a conversation, especially when your spouse is not preoccupied (driving in the car together is often an ideal time), by saying something like, "I've been feeling kind of discouraged by a situation at work this week." That's all it takes. Your spouse will likely pick up on this quickly and follow up with some questions. But try not to make it a guessing game. Disclose as much as you can, especially your feelings. If it makes you terribly uncomfortable to do so, you can say that to your spouse as well. "Just talking about my feelings on this is tough for me," you might say, "but I want to do this because I know it's healthy for our marriage." As we said, this is a true gift to your spouse.

Modify Your Plan

This can be another tough pill for you to swallow, but changing your plan is sure to convey your love to your spouse. Why? Because you don't often do this. You like to stick to your plan for a vacation, or what time to meet, or the holidays, or where you're having dinner, or when you're getting a pet, or you name it. You don't like your plans to change. It jolts your spirit and knocks you out of alignment.

That's exactly why gracefully modifying your plan to accommodate something your spouse desires is such a loving thing for you to do. The person with an Optimist Love Style or Leader Love Style can change plans on a dime. They like the potential reward that the unplanned opportunity can afford. They hold their plans loosely to take advantage of a new prospect. Chances are good that your spouse would love it if you would, on occasion, flex your plan to do the same thing.

If you scheduled getting your grocery shopping done on a particular afternoon and your spouse says, "Hey, Tom and Sarah just called to see if we'd join them at Spenser's for a cup of that delicious soup they serve on Saturday. They bought a new car and they want to take us for a spin," inside, your heart feels torn with tension. You want to get your task done. You think to yourself that you can see their new car later, after you've done your shopping. Besides, you're not all that crazy about the soup at Spenser's. But your spouse is noticeably excited and motivated to go. "I told them I'd call them back in a few minutes to let them know if it would work for us," your spouse says.

> True strength lies in submission which permits one to dedicate his life, through devotion, to something beyond himself.
>
> *Henry Miller*

So what do you do? If you want to be a more loving spouse, you say, "I was planning on shopping while the store is stocked, but it sounds like this could be fun. Do you think we could go and then do the shopping afterward?"

That's all it takes. A simple modification of your plan is a concrete way of being a better spouse. It won't always come easy, but it *will* always come with a reward for your marriage.

Learn to Say No

There are countless worthy requests that come your way. Your friends and colleagues have come to count on you as the go-to person when they need a little help. After all, you are competent and agreeable. You're pleasant and enjoyable. And you're easy to get along with. Why wouldn't people come to you with their requests? "Would you help organize the church picnic?" "Would you water my plants while I'm gone?" "Would you lend me that book when you're done reading it?" "Would you meet my friend for a little mentoring?" "Would you...?" And on and on, the requests for your time and talents go, eating up your days and adding to your stress—especially when you've said "yes" way too many times.

Your spouse has probably asked you on more than one occasion to put a clamp on your willingness to help "everyone who asks." You've probably tried. But if this is still an issue in your marriage, if you know it is disconcerting to your spouse, consider giving it a better effort.

Here's what you can do. Begin by realizing that saying *no* helps you prioritize the things that are important to you. You'll gain time that you can commit to the things that you really want to do, such as leaving work at a reasonable hour. Examine your current obligations and overall priorities before making any new commitments. Ask yourself if the new commitment is important to you. If it's something that you feel strongly about, by all means do it. But also ask yourself if the new activity that you're considering is a short- or long-term commitment. Taking an afternoon to bake a batch of cookies for the school bake sale will take far less of your precious time than heading up the school fundraising committee for an entire year. If an activity is going to end up being an eventual source of stress in your life—especially for the long term—and if it is going to take you away from your marriage, take a pass. How? By first complimenting the person or the group's effort, then saying that you'll need some time to talk it over with your spouse. Tell them that you will email your reply. This is sometimes easier than saying *no* immediately and in person. Then, do as you said and talk it over with your spouse. If you decide it's best to pass, send an email right away that says, "I'm sorry, but I'm unable to commit at this time." That's all. You don't need to explain.

As you begin to turn down things that are taking you away from your marriage, your spouse will feel more and more loved. Especially since you are including him or her in the decision-making process.

Join in the Excitement

We know this doesn't come naturally to you, but even the slightest lean toward a show of enthusiasm and excitement would bring joy to your spouse. When your partner receives good news, maybe about a promotion at work or a score on the golf course, and shares the news with you, consider

> All we are saying is give peace a chance.
>
> *John Lennon*

your normal reaction. Sure, you are happy about the news. Sure, you say, "Congratulations." You say, "That's terrific." But, compared to most people, your show of excitement is, well, not very exciting. You know that.

Reed felt the same way. As a Devoted Spouse, he had a naturally underdeveloped expression of excitement. He always felt he was expressing more excitement than he really was. His wife knew better. She would share some good news that made her happy, and Reed would say, without changing his demeanor, something like, "That's wonderful." Period. He wouldn't elaborate or celebrate. That was it. It didn't matter if the news regarded something big or small. His expression over completing a jigsaw puzzle was the same as winning a drawing for a free refrigerator. Either way, he'd simply say it was wonderful and go on about his day. His wife was routinely depleted of her own excitement, until she came to expect a less-than-enthusiastic response from Reed. So she would always tell her sister about her good news before telling Reed. This irritated Reed, but, of course, he didn't express it. What else could his optimistic wife do?

Do you agree? And don't you want your spouse to come to you first with any good news? Of course you do. Why not try to amp up your enthusiasm with a warm and genuine hug? Why not say something like, "This is fantastic news! We need to celebrate! This is really special." We know it's not in your nature to do this automatically. We're just suggesting that you try. If you can give it some genuine effort, even just enough to bring about a minor increased expression of excitement, your spouse will deeply appreciate it. And the more often you do it, the easier it will become.

Share an Activity

The ancient Greek philosopher Aristotle said, "The quality of life is determined by its activities." That may not be a sentiment you share, but if your spouse has been longing to share an activity with you and you've been resisting, give it some serious consideration. Maybe your spouse wants to share a bike ride or a walk around the neighborhood. Maybe it's a game of tennis or antique shopping. Don't make your spouse beg for it. Surprise your partner with a ready willingness to go.

Paula, a true Validator who prized doing nothing with her free time, knew her husband wanted to rent a kayak

at a nearby lake. He'd been talking about it all summer. Paula dragged her feet on the idea because it just
wasn't something she wanted to do. Her husband eventually went kayaking on his own. When he returned home,
he went on and on

> If we have no peace, it is because we have forgotten that we belong to each other.
>
> *Mother Teresa*

about how great it was. "It's so relaxing and freeing to
be out there on the water," he told Paula. But she interpreted that as pressure to join him, so she resisted even
more. "That all sounds good for you, but it's not my kind
of thing," she'd say. The topic was dead. He didn't mention it anymore. The next Saturday, however, when her
husband was again going out to kayak by himself, she
volunteered to try it with him. "You would have thought
I'd given him a gold bar or something," Paula confessed.
"I literally had no idea that this would mean so much to
him. I hadn't made him that happy for a very long time."

You can do the same thing. It doesn't take much. If
you've been resisting a shared activity that your spouse
wants you to do, consider an about-face and do it. You'll
double the fun for your partner, and it will surely bring you
closer together.

Where to Go from Here

Well, there you have it, a summary of your personal Love
Style as the Devoted Spouse. Of course, you're likely to
have a secondary Love Style as indicated on your report
from the online L.O.V.E. Style Assessment. So feel free to
move next to the chapter describing that style.

If your spouse has completed the online L.O.V.E. Style
Assessment, we also suggest you turn to the chapter that

summarizes his or her style(s). Even though it is written to your spouse, it will help you gain a deeper understanding of your partner.

Of course, you may find it interesting to read the other chapters in this section of the book as well. Even if they don't apply directly to your own Love Style, they can sometimes serve as a helpful way of contrasting your style to the others.

Once you are ready, you'll want to eventually move to Part Three of the book, where you'll learn how you can put your specific Love Styles to work for you.

For Reflection and Discussion

1. How well does this chapter describe you? Give it a percentage ranking and explain why. Be specific. In other words, back up your ranking with a few specific examples.

2. As you consider how you are hardwired for love, what is one specific thing that your spouse could do to better love you? Why might it be difficult for him or her to do this?

WORKBOOK EXERCISE
for the Devoted Spouse

If you're electing to use the optional his/her interactive workbooks, you'll want to turn to the exercise designed specifically for you to apply this chapter to your marriage. It contains several brief exercises that are sure to make this information come alive in your relationship.

EVALUATOR: THE CAREFUL SPOUSE

Some emotions don't make a lot of noise.
Caring is real faint—like a heartbeat.

Anonymous

WITH AN EVALUATOR Love Style, you are Project-Oriented and Slow-Paced. The combination of these two dispositions makes you a Careful Spouse. Note where you land in the four Love Style quadrants:

We'll begin this chapter by exploring your deepest needs. These are the needs you must have met in order to function at your optimal level—especially in your marriage. Speaking of your optimal level, we'll

	Project-Oriented	People-Oriented
Fast-Paced	Leader The Take-Charge Spouse	Optimist The Encouraging Spouse
Slow-Paced	Evaluator The Careful Spouse	Validator The Devoted Spouse

move from there to "You at Your Best," looking at the five traits that emerge from within you when you are doing well and in your groove. Of course, we will also take a look at "You at Your Worst." We'll look at the five traits that come into view when your deeper needs are not being met.

> The surest hindrance of success is to have too high a standard of refinement in our own minds, or too high an opinion of the judgment of the public. He who is determined not to be satisfied with anything short of perfection will never do anything to please himself or others.
>
> *William Hazlitt*

Next, we'll turn to "How You're Hardwired for Love." In other words, well explore how your unique combination of personality traits blend together to create who you are as a spouse and what you are looking for in your relationship.

This will take us to how you function within "The Five Domains of Real-Life Marriage." These include communication, conflict, sex, finances, and free time. We'll take a close look at how you approach each one.

Finally, we'll give you some practical ways to "Better Love Your Spouse." After you understand your own deep needs and how they shape your approach to marriage, you are poised to become much better at loving your partner at a deeper level.

Before we jump in, we want you to keep in mind that you will likely read something here or there that you don't agree with. In other words, you might think that a particular trait we're exploring doesn't come close to describing you. That's okay. Don't let that interfere with the content you find helpful. Assuming you've taken the online L.O.V.E. Style Assessment, you already know that your personality is too complex to fit neatly into a box. In all likelihood, you are a combination of Love Styles where one is more dominant than the other. That being the case, we don't expect every description in this chapter to fit you perfectly.

Now, take a deep breath. Keep an open mind. Tune into what rings true to your experience and set aside what doesn't. And take your time as you discover your own Love Style.

Your Deepest Needs

As a person with an Evaluator Love Style, you want nothing short of perfection. It's a tall order, of course, but you're hardwired to come as close to it as possible. Take, for example, your decision-making process. If you're making a decision about buying a new car or taking up a new hobby, you'll do your research. You are determined to make the right and best decision. You won't settle for anything less.

You're going to evaluate your options. You'll appraise each possibility. You'll take your time. You won't be rushed. You'll go to the experts for input and advice. You'll ask probing questions, and you'll take notes. You're likely to agonize over your decision—the more important, the more agonizing—continuing to weigh the pros and cons. Once you've made your decision, it's going to be tough for anyone to change your mind. Your decisions are based on facts, not opinions. And you stick by them.

Your evaluative nature reveals another deep need: quality. It's not that you necessarily appreciate quality items (though you likely do), but that you aspire to live and maintain a quality life. You want your days on this planet to be of value and worth. You want them to count.

You seek excellence—whether it's professionally or personally. You're not one to settle for mediocrity at any level. You have a deep need to do the right thing, the right way. You don't like anything to interfere with fulfilling this expectation, either. You follow due process—even if it takes time. You patiently read directions to be sure you're doing things correctly.

> Quality is not an act, it is a habit.
>
> *Aristotle*

**The Careful Spouse's Motto:
Anything worth doing is worth doing right.**

You at Your Best

Your strivings for quality, excellence, and perfection tend to bring with them numerous traits that add value to your marriage. Here are some of them.

Orderly

The Careful Spouse is typically well organized. Everything has its proper place. You're structured and sequential. You're usually neat, tidy, and orderly. On occasion, the Careful Spouse may keep things a bit cluttered to the point of appearing disorganized. But, if this is you, you're certain to know exactly what's in your seemingly cluttered piles. Even in your apparent disorder, you're orderly.

Conscientious

You're often painstakingly thorough. Compared to others, you can be meticulous about thinking through every aspect of a project or responsibility you have. People know they can count on you to do whatever you are doing the right way. Your competence is rarely in question because you so carefully execute your thorough plans.

Scheduled

You run a tight ship when it comes to your calendar. You know what you're doing at nearly any moment of any given day. You have a system for making sure you're prepared for your appointments and that they aren't missed.

You're careful not to overschedule, sometimes accounting for a buffer that gives you leeway in your schedule, but you are thoroughly planned and programmed. You're almost always on time. If you aren't, it's because you had an understandable reason—not because you simply "forgot."

> Quality, quality, quality: never waver from it, even when you don't see how you can afford to keep it up. When you compromise, you become a commodity and then you die.
>
> *Gary Hirshberg*

Purposeful

Not only are you scheduled, but also your appointments have a purpose. That is, you have a mission that is focused and resolute. High standards motivate you. Simply keeping the status quo is not enough to get you going. You don't want to simply "kill time." You need a purpose that is philosophically consistent with your life's call. You don't meander through your days; you typically move with an intentional pace for a specific and deliberate purpose.

Factual

As a Careful Spouse, you value accurate information. You like to know the facts more than the feelings. You deal with precision, accuracy, and exactness.

You don't like to guess. You don't like to go on hearsay. You want to know what is certain—or at least the statistical odds—so that you can act from a base of solid information that is reliable and tested. You're more comfortable with graphs and charts than blogs and opinions.

> Intelligent or not, we all make mistakes and perhaps the intelligent mistakes are the worst, because so much careful thought has gone into them.
>
> *Peter Ustinov*

You at Your Worst

It's true that our greatest strengths can have a dark side. So let's take a look at yours. When you are at your worst—when your primary needs aren't getting met—you tend to demonstrate the following traits:

Obsessive

If your standards aren't being met, you become preoccupied with what might have improved your circumstances. You begin saying, "If only …" and "What if …" If you don't meet a goal or you feel like you dropped the ball, you ruminate on it. You play it over in your mind. You fixate on the nuances of things until they consume you. You are prone to get caught up in the details and lose sight of the big picture because you're obsessed with something smaller that didn't go your way.

Critical

When something is substandard in your eyes—whether it be a restaurant, a film, or a conversation—you become negative, disapproving, and judgmental. You can also move into this critical mode when someone, including your spouse, opposes your ideas or decisions. You may not always verbalize your displeasure when this occurs, but people around you pick it up. When you disapprove, people know it.

Moody

Almost everyone can be a bit moody from time to time, but you lean into this more than most. When your deeper needs are not being met, you may even use your irritability and grumpy disposition to manipulate your spouse and others. If you want someone's behavior or opinion to change, your moodiness can become an almost unconscious tactic for getting what you want. To say the least, you become temperamental when things don't go your way. In these moments, you tend to be in a funk.

Suspicious

The more your need for perfection is unacknowledged, the more skeptical and pessimistic you become. That is, when you are feeling more out of control, the more suspicious you are of ideas, programs, and people—including your spouse. He or she may find it especially challenging to convince you of something (how much something cost, the amount of time it takes, etc.) when you are in this zone. Why? Because you are

> Ruth and I don't have a perfect marriage, but we have a great one. How can I say two things that seem so contradictory? In a perfect marriage, everything is always the finest and best imaginable; like a Greek statue, the proportions are exact and the finish is unblemished. Who knows any human being like that? To expect perfection in each other is unrealistic.
>
> *Billy Graham*

especially cynical and doubtful about either the message or the messenger.

Rigid

Because you strive for quality, you can become more unbending than most. You can hold firm to what you expect. You may, for example, be especially strict and stern about what is unacceptable to you—whether it's your overcooked eggs or your child's misbehavior. You can border on legalistic and judgmental in these moments. Mostly, you are unyielding over what is tolerable or good enough.

How You're Hardwired to Love

You have high ideals for your marriage. You want to have the very best marriage possible and, if you don't get too discouraged by some aspect of your relationship, you're generally motivated to work at that. You certainly don't want a mediocre marriage, and you don't want the "typical" marriage either. You want your relationship with your spouse to excel, and you have some pretty clear ideas about how to achieve that—whether or not your spouse agrees with you.

> Perfection is achieved, not when there is nothing more to add, but when there is nothing left to take away.
>
> *Antoine de Saint-Exupery*

More than most, you analyze your marriage. You evaluate and question what each of you is doing in the relationship. You carefully assess and appraise the status of your marriage. For you, love is not just something you feel, it's something you improve.

Because you care so deeply about your marriage, you can become easily hurt by your spouse. All it takes is a sign of disapproval or a word of criticism for you to feel let down or wounded by your partner. Your spouse has, no doubt, adapted to this sensitivity in you and is probably cautious not to pass judgment on you.

When things are going well, when you feel pretty good about your standards being met, you are a conscientious partner who likes to know what your spouse wants from you—the more detailed, the better. And you'll work hard to meet those expectations and desires. In fact, you derive pleasure from knowing precisely what you can do to make your spouse feel more appreciated and loved.

You'll also focus on positive solutions when you recognize a problem in the relationship. In other words, you won't complain about something as long as you feel there is something you can do to improve it, even if it takes some time. When you do improve it, you want your spouse to acknowledge that and appreciate your efforts. On the other hand, you feel down in the dumps if you sense your spouse is not working equally as hard on doing the same for you in return.

As a Careful Spouse, you demonstrate your love by being practical, thorough, punctual, dependable, deliberate, and responsible. You, more than most people, give careful attention to your marriage, ensuring that it is the best it can be.

How the Careful Spouse Defines Love
Love is…having time to gather my thoughts
and feel good about a decision.

You and the Five Domains of Real-Life Marriage

Every marriage, regardless of its stage, has specific domains that can become sticking points between a husband and wife. This is especially true for couples who have not explored how their personal Love Styles impact and shape each one of these domains. These include: communication, conflict, sex, finances, and free time.

Here's how you approach each one.

Your Approach to Communication

You like a sensible conversation, especially when it's deep, serious, and intellectual. You like to focus on the facts, but you'll also probe for the "hidden meaning" behind words. You'll often ask specific questions of your partner as you seek to understand at a deep level. You'll sometimes ask the same question again and again until you find the reassurance, feedback, and reasons for something.

In almost all your conversations with your spouse, you need information and time to carefully consider whatever is being discussed.

Your Approach to Conflict

Many of your fights are the result of feeling criticized or because you have read something into your spouse's motivations. Once the disagreement begins, you tend to be very rigid and overly detailed when quarreling with your

> Be careful as a naked man climbin' a barbed wire fence.
> *Cowboy Proverb*

spouse. That is, you will quote what he or she said—even from days or weeks earlier—and cite specific instances to back up your points. Instead of verbalizing your conflict, you may even be apt to write a long note that gives a detailed and logical explanation of your grievance. As a tactic, you may also ask questions, much like an attorney, that trap your partner in a corner, proving how you are correct and your spouse is wrong. You don't enjoy fighting, but you generally keep your wits about you in the process, unless you withdraw in a morose and moody way.

Your Approach to Sex and Intimacy

You tend to approach sexuality in your marriage with a sense of schedule. That is, your sexual desires are relatively predictable. Your spouse generally knows what to expect. You also tend to "have sex" more than you "make love." It's something on your list and you're intentional about it, rather than just letting it happen when the mood evolves. Yet, you like to take your time and get it "right." You also like to know exactly what your spouse likes from you in your passionate times together. And you like to be appreciated for your intimate efforts.

Your Approach to Finances

More than any other style, you are highly organized in financial matters. You almost know to the penny how much money you have. In all likelihood, your paper currency is likely to face the same direction in your billfold or purse. You're risk-averse with your finances. You fear making a wrong financial decision. You not only want to avoid a mistake, but also you want to be sure you are not viewed as incompetent. If you have the means, you're likely to use a money manager or accountant, but you'll still want to verify what they are doing with your money. If you don't have outside help, you'll certainly do research on your own, asking professionals for their opinions.

Your Approach to Free Time

You are studious and would often rather read or study or create than interact with others—sometimes even your spouse. You likely have specialized hobbies that require intention and skill. When you spend free time together with your spouse, you want it to have a purpose.

You want to accomplish something. If you're into photography, for example, you don't want to simply take pictures to record a memory. You want to take "perfect" pictures that you can proudly display. You want to check a goal or an accomplishment off your list. In other words, you want your free time together to be useful and practical.

> Be careful what you set your heart upon—for it will surely be yours.
>
> *James Arthur Baldwin*

How You Can Better Love Your Spouse

As a person who likes to be particularly careful—a person who is focused on taking the time to do things right—there are several specific actions you can take that are sure to improve your marriage. So we dedicate the closing section of this chapter to highlighting these actions and wishing you the very best in becoming a better spouse.

Lighten Up

Let's face it. You can be pretty serious. Striving for perfection will do that to a person. Your inclination to be analytical, orderly, precise, scheduled, detailed, discerning, controlled, and purposeful—whew!—can take a bit of a toll on even the most agreeable spouse.

Consider what a little more laughter might do for your marriage. "A cheerful heart," as Proverbs says, "is good medicine." The soul of your marriage could likely benefit from a dose of humor, don't you think? The poet E.E. Cummings says, "The most wasted of all days is one without laughter." Why waste another day of your marriage without bringing a genuine smile to your spouse's face?

Here's the good news. It's easier than you think. Why? Because all you need to do to crack your spouse up is just one thing that's a bit out of the norm for your controlled and detailed demeanor. For example, try wearing a hat to breakfast. It's sure to get a smile. Or put a stuffed animal in your refrigerator for your spouse to discover. You don't need to become David Letterman. You simply need to do something your spouse isn't expecting.

Few things are more endearing than a sense of humor. Jay Leno says, "You can't stay mad at somebody who makes you laugh." And the great Bill Cosby says, "If you can find humor in anything, you can survive it." That's especially true for you because you take life so seriously. Bringing more laughter into your marriage will not only benefit your marriage and make your spouse feel more loved, but also it will help you too.

Relax the Rules

You may not perceive it this way, but there is a pretty strong chance that your spouse sometimes feels like you have an invisible rule book for your marriage. Your partner likely sometimes fears breaking a rule that you have created. Why? Because of your high standards. Your lofty expectations create rules and regulations for your relationship. Your spouse knows that if a rule is broken there's likely a price to pay. It might be a sharp criticism, or it might be some sulking. Whatever it is, your partner wants to avoid it.

What would happen in your marriage, what would it do for your partner's spirit, if you were to relax a rule here or there? Let's get specific. What "rule" seems to get your spouse into the most trouble in your home? Maybe it's leaving a coat on the back of a chair. Maybe it's messing up the pillows on the couch. Maybe it's talking too long on the phone. Only you and your spouse know.

Do you have one in mind? Here's our challenge. Try to relax just that one rule for one month. In other words, bite your tongue about that one thing the next time your spouse does it. And don't silently sulk, either. Of course, it's going to be tough. You're fearful that if you don't enforce the rule your spouse will start breaking your other rules. But that's not the case. Instead, your spouse is almost sure to acknowledge how loving you are—because he or she already knows that it irritates you.

No pressure. Just something to consider as a practical way for you to better love your spouse.

Excuse the Incorrect Details

One of your general tendencies is to correct the details in the conversations you have with your spouse. Or for that matter, to correct the details anytime you hear your spouse speaking with someone else. Consider the following scenario of your spouse talking to friends over a cup of coffee:

"Last Thursday I was coming up Westlake Avenue and saw Jerry walking out of his office. I honked, but I don't think …"

"Honey," you speak up, "Jerry's office is on Denny, not Westlake."

"Well, whatever, I was downtown and saw him," your spouse continues. "He has this huge potted plant and I'm guessing …"

"Wait a second," you interrupt again. "You were at your mom's last Thursday, so it had to be Friday."

Do you see a little bit of yourself in this scenario? Do you notice that you sometimes interrupt to be sure your spouse's facts are straight? You may not even be aware of doing this. But most Careful Spouses can't help but to correct misinformation. Unfortunately, this comes across as inconsiderate and even rude to nearly everyone else, especially when you are correcting your own spouse.

If you'd like to curb this distressing tendency, it's quite simple. It has to do with increasing your level of awareness. A tip that's helpful to many, especially in public settings, is to simply devise a little signal that your spouse can use to let you know

> There are some enterprises in which a careful disorderliness is the true method.
>
> *Herman Melville*

you're doing it. Your spouse might simply give a gentle tug on his or her earlobe, for example. Let your spouse know that you want to improve this behavior and decide on the signal together.

Even expressing the desire to change this annoying habit will be a loving gesture your spouse will appreciate.

Allow for Interruptions

Even though you generally feel free to interrupt your spouse to make a correction or comment, you are likely to detest being interrupted yourself—especially when you are working on a project, taking a phone call, or just reading a story in the newspaper. You like closure. You like to have things neat and tidy. You live sequentially, where one thing gets wrapped up before moving to the next. You typically don't want an interruption of any kind to throw off your linear progression of tasks.

Of course, life doesn't always work that way. You can do your best to minimize interruptions, but they're inevitable. Your spouse or your child needs your attention right now—whether you think it's justifiable or not. And they should have the right to interrupt you when you're needed without suffering a formidable consequence from you.

So if, in retrospect, you think you may have laid down the law a little too hard on your spouse for interrupting you, perhaps you could express your desire to lighten up on this behavior. You could say something like: "I know that I can be pretty gruff when you interrupt me while I'm working on an email I'm writing, and I want you to know that I don't want to be that kind of spouse. I don't know if I'm going to change overnight, but I want you to know that you're more important to me than a task like that. I want you to feel free to let me know if you need me for something."

> This is the very perfection of a man, to find out his own imperfection.
>
> *Saint Augustine*

A little statement like that will speak volumes to your spouse. You probably don't even know how appreciative your partner will be to hear words like this coming out of your mouth. And here's something good to know. Your spouse is likely to be even more sensitive to your need not to be interrupted and far less likely to be resentful of it. In a real sense, you'll both win with this loving strategy.

Power Down the Criticism

One of the toughest things you might ever do to create a more loving marriage is to work on putting a clamp on criticism. This tendency, when your deeper needs are not getting met, is so ingrained in you that it will require some serious discipline. Truthfully, it is likely to mellow the longer you are married. But it's worth the effort at any point for you to power down your critical comments toward your spouse.

Much of the time you may not even be aware of how often and intensely you utter critical comments. But if you're like most Careful Spouses, you do this frequently. You say things like: "You put these forks in here the wrong way," or, "Would you quit touching my pen?" or even "Don't you know how to put a shirt on a hanger?" You might say, "What did you do to make this so messy?" or "You're not in the left lane," or "I can't believe you said that to him," or "You bought the wrong kind of dressing," or finally, "Would you back off and give me some breathing room?"

If you find yourself being more critical than you'd like, try these steps. First, apologize to your spouse. Say something like, "I know that I can be more critical than some people, and I want you to know that I realize this isn't always easy to live with. I'm really sorry." Second, ask your spouse when they feel like you are most critical. You might be able to locate specific times (just before dinner, when you are hungry, for example) or particular circumstances (when your monthly report at work is due). Next, ask your spouse for suggestions on ways you could curb it. Don't make it their responsibility, but invite input. You may discover that what you thought was critical isn't so much to your spouse and that what you haven't given much thought to really is. He or she can guide you a bit on how to lighten up.

> Endeavor to be always patient of the faults and imperfections of others for thou hast many faults and imperfections of thine own.
>
> *Thomas à Kempis*

Finally, invite your spouse to hold you accountable in one particular area where the critical comments hurt the most. Don't try to instantly diminish all criticism. It's too tough. Start by focusing on the area your spouse suggests.

Where to Go from Here

Well, there you have it, a summary of your personal Love Style as the Careful Spouse. Of course, you're likely to have a secondary Love Style as indicated on your report from the online L.O.V.E. Style Assessment. So feel free to move next to the chapter describing that style.

If your spouse has completed the online L.O.V.E. Style Assessment, we also suggest you turn to the chapter that summarizes his or her style(s). Even though it is written to your spouse, it will help you gain a deeper understanding of your partner.

Of course, you may find it interesting to read the other chapters in this section of the book as well. Even if they don't apply directly to your own Love Style, they can sometimes serve as a helpful way of contrasting your style to the others.

Once you are ready, you'll want to eventually move to Part Three of the book where you'll learn how you can put your specific Love Styles to work for you.

For Reflection and Discussion

1. How well does this chapter describe you? Give it a percentage ranking and explain why. Be specific. In other words, back up your ranking with a few specific examples.

2. As you consider how you are hardwired for love, what is one specific thing that your spouse could do to better love you? Why might it be difficult for your partner to do this?

3. When it comes to how you can better love your spouse, which item in this chapter is something you can immediately put into practice and how? Also which item will be most challenging for you and why?

WORKBOOK EXERCISE
for the Careful Spouse

If you're electing to use the optional his/her interactive workbooks, you'll want to turn to the exercise designed specifically for you to apply this chapter to your marriage. It contains several brief exercises that are sure to make this information come alive in your relationship.

PART THREE

PUTTING YOUR LOVE STYLES TO WORK FOR YOU

NOW IT'S TIME to turn the tables. We've looked at *your* personal Love Style, but what about your partner's? In this section we explore how you can better relate to your spouse by understanding his or her particular Love Style. We devote a chapter to each of the four styles, so feel free to turn directly to the chapter that pertains to your spouse. Here, you will find a clear explanation of what you can expect from your spouse, what your spouse fears most, and how to love your spouse in ways that will be especially meaningful to your partner. In addition, we'll look at what you can do to maintain your own emotional health in relation to your spouse's Love Style.

Once you've had a chance to read that chapter, we also recommend that you peruse the chapter that your spouse will read about you. Review it together and underscore points that may be especially helpful for your spouse to understand about how to love you best.

IF YOU'RE MARRIED TO A LEADER

Follow your bliss.

Joseph Campbell

REMEMBER THE OLD school yard game "Follow the Leader"? First, a leader or "head of the line," is chosen, then the children all line up behind the leader. The leader moves around, and all the children have to mimic the leader's actions. Any players who mess up or do not do what the leader does are out of the game.

Chances are you're pretty good at this game, even if you haven't signed up for it. In fact, for you, it has morphed from a game into a way of married life. Why? Because you are married to a powerful personality. You're married to a Leader, and leaders need followers. Of the four Love Styles, the one you're married to is the most commanding, dominant, and driven.

Rick, married nine years, has all the subtlety of a freight train. He is full of bluster and bravado, whether he is at home or at the office. And his lack of tact, coupled with clumsy attempts at communication, frequently alienate him not only from his coworkers but also from his spouse. Rick blurts out critical comments, never realizing the damage he does to others' feelings: "What's wrong with your hair?" "You're out in left field again; get back to the main issue," or "You can't seem to get anything right today, can you?"

If you're married to a high-octane Leader, you've probably heard more than your fair share of statements like these. You don't need us to tell you that your spouse is a Take-Charge person.

But what you may find helpful here are some of the most proven and effective strategies for making your relationship with a purpose-driven spouse the very best it can be. We want to reveal exactly what you can expect from your spouse, what your spouse fears most, and what you need to do—in specific terms—to love your spouse successfully. Finally, we show you how you can stay strong and healthy when married to a Take-Charge Spouse.

What You Can Expect from a Leader: The Take-Charge Spouse

If merit badges were given out in marriage, you would likely earn one in long-suffering. Why? Because you're married to a person who is often distracted, irritable, and impatient. That requires you to endure countless occasions when you feel inadequate. Impatience and irritability from a spouse send a message that you don't measure up—that you're not fast enough, smart enough, or helpful enough. The message is not necessarily intentional, but it can be excruciating when you're on the receiving end of it.

As a result, you are bound to sometimes feel like a second-class partner. When your spouse is at his or her worst, you can count on feeling underappreciated and unimportant. In addition to feeling as if you don't matter, you may also feel like you are actually making life more difficult for your spouse. And nobody likes to feel like that. No well-intentioned husband or wife deserves to feel like that.

On the flip side, when your spouse is at his or her best, you can expect to feel energized, excited, and uplifted. In these moments, you're sure to feel like the proverbial wind beneath your partner's wings. There's no mistaking it. Just as the Take-Charge Spouse isn't shy about noticing your foibles, he or she is also outspoken and proud of your contributions—especially when your contributions make life better. That's when your spouse will sing your praises the loudest.

When your spouse's needs are not being met, you can expect to be bossed around a bit. His or her irritability will zero in on any lack of effort on your part and will quickly label you as lazy or inept. Your spouse will manifest a managerial attitude. He or she will supervise you with an air of superiority. In the absence of his or her fulfilled needs, you can also expect more than a few snide comments to emerge. For example, "Did you already clean this? If you did, you need to do it again because you missed most of it."

On the other hand, when your partner's needs are being met, your spouse is likely to serve as your North Star, providing you with a secure sense of direction and comfort. Sure, the Take-Charge Spouse inspires a busy life that seems to overflow with activity and endless distractions, but you're never bored and you always have a sense that the busyness is leading you in a positive and purposeful direction.

What Your Spouse Wants Most from You

♥ Agreement and deference
♥ Facts more than feelings
♥ Support of his or her plan

♥ Anything that saves time
♥ Direct communication (to the point)
♥ Logic and objectivity
♥ Competition (in playing games)

What Your Take-Charge Spouse Fears Most

Imagine what life would be like if everything you wanted and every goal you hoped to achieve was dictated by the winds of fate or by other people's whims. The prospect of such powerlessness would be terrifying. Yet your spouse, at a deep level, lives with this fear on a daily basis. That's what propels the compulsion to control.

Sondra likes to run the show in her marriage. She's married to a relatively passive man who is comfortable playing second fiddle, so Sondra seems to take the lead. When they go out to eat, she not only selects the restaurant, but also often requests a different table than the one the hostess offers. She may even suggest what her husband should order off the menu. Why does Sondra take charge of something so mundane? The answer is found at a more subconscious than conscious level. Deep down, Sondra fears losing control.

That's exactly what your Take-Charge Spouse fears. Your partner is afraid of resistance and opposition from you that would make it more difficult to obtain a goal. Not only that, the Leader Spouse fears losing your appreciation for taking the lead. The Leader sometimes worries that you don't value his or her contribution to the marriage. If that worry takes root in your relationship, you're guaranteed to have a spouse who feels wounded. The Take-Charge Spouse feels most deeply hurt when you resist the Leader's influence and when you withdraw your appreciation.

How to Love a Take-Charge Spouse

Everybody wants a happy marriage. And a happy marriage is the result of two people operating at the top of their game—where both spouses are functioning at their best, with the strengths from their inborn personalities in full play. With this in mind, here are a few specifics that will help you insure that your spouse can operate from the positive aspects of his or her God-given personality traits. It will also help you honor your spouse's Love Style.

Get on Board or Get Out of the Way

Being married to a Take-Charge Spouse is like riding a bicycle—if you don't pedal forward, you'll fall off. Your spouse is on the move and if you don't move in the same direction, your partner will, figuratively, run right over you. That means that one of the best ways of loving your spouse

> He that complies against his will is of his own opinion still.
> *Samuel Butler*

is to get on board with his or her plans. This doesn't mean that you have to buy into every detail, it simply means sharing in the enthusiasm for the general direction.

You can do this by saying things like, "I don't know how you come up with so much energy, but I'm all for it," or, "I love it that you want to do this. I'm going to be cheering you on every step of the way." That's all it takes for your spouse to feel that you are on board. Your partner will love you for it.

Look Beneath the Surface

Successfully loving your spouse depends, in great measure, on finding out what the Leader really wants from you at a particular moment. You can do that by asking yourself a question such as, "Is my partner trying to make me verify that he is right, important, recognized, appreciated, powerful?" In other words, *What's my partner feeling below the surface?*

To love your partner effectively, you have to figure out how to give in to the Take-Charge Spouse without compromising your own needs. If your spouse is anxious about an important phone call he is waiting to receive, for example, he might snap at you for putting your feet on the coffee table. "Why do you do that?" he might demand. "I've told you before how upsetting that is to me." Rather than accuse him of being irrational and petty, put yourself in his shoes and ask yourself what he really needs. Your response might then be, "I'm sorry, I bet you're anxious about that call you're waiting for."

A simple statement about what might be going on beneath the surface can be a soothing touch on the soul of your worried spouse. And it will help you weather the controlling storm without getting drenched.

Concede When You Can

Here's the deal: Because you're married to a strong personality, you're going to have situations in your relationship when you are up against a powerful force that is not about to back down. Our advice is to choose your battles wisely. We're not talking about being a doormat or not having a spine. You don't have to be a wimp. There are times when you definitely need to stand your own ground and not budge, but make sure those times are on issues that really matter and aren't just a means to gain more turf in a power struggle.

> **Better bend than break.**
> *Scottish proverb*

This might be a tough pill to swallow, especially if you are an Evaluator. But all we are saying with this suggestion is that you try to make your marriage as easy as it can be by going along with your spouse's Leader Love-Style when it doesn't matter as much to you.

For example, your spouse may feel dead set on eating at a particular restaurant that's not your favorite. Granted, you may not enjoy it as much as your first choice, but if your spouse is insistent and you can live with the choice on this occasion, give up the fight. Let it go. Don't whine or moan. Choose to put your energy into a tug-of-war on issues that matter most to you.

Dwight Eisenhower, a strong personality himself, said, "Pull the string, and it will follow wherever you wish. Push it, and it will go nowhere at all." The point is that you'll get nowhere by trying to push your partner. So when it's time to wield the force of your opinion and desires, make a logical case for your perspective rather than challenging your spouse's perspective.

Make Your Partner's Life Easier

Okay, do you want one surefire way to make your Take-Charge Spouse feel more loved? Here it is. Ask this simple question with a genuine heart: *What can I do to make your day easier?* Now, don't ask it unless you intend to make good on it. But if you follow up with the favor asked, your spouse will truly draw closer to you. The Leader Love Style is all about productivity. So when you make the day easier, when you help carry the load or remove some obstacles—even a little—you are meeting a deep need and you are sure to be appreciated.

As we said, be prepared to follow through, because if you simply ask and then complain about not being able to deliver, you've made things worse. You've sent a message of resentment or inadequacy. Take comfort in the fact that the requests your spouse will make are typically not that big. Your spouse might say, "To be honest, it would really help if you could give me just one hour of uninterrupted time to work on this report after dinner." Or, "I would love it if you could pick up the kids today even though it's my turn."

The goal is to lighten the load, relieve the burden, and smooth out the path—just a little. You do that on a relatively routine basis for your spouse, and you'll soon see just how indispensible and deeply appreciated you become.

Confirm the Complaints

One of the great temptations in being married to a Leader is to tune your spouse out. Most children, for example, have mastered this strategy. We psychologists call it "mommy deafness," a sudden, temporary inability to hear any request mom makes. Indeed, children can notice the tinkle of an ice-cream truck a block away, but they can't hear Mom right in front of them.

You may be tempted to do the same thing with your partner, but you'll miss something important if you tune out your Take-Charge Spouse. Why? Because sometimes you'll find help in their critical comments! In referring to the critics in his life, missionary and theologian E. Stanley Jones said, "They are the unpaid watchmen of my soul."[9] The best way to keep your ears open is to restate your partner's complaint to get confirmation. After hearing the complaint, say, "Let me be sure I've understood you. You are saying …," then repeat the criticism in your own words. Next, ask, "Did I get that right?" If you're not quite receiving the message that's being sent, ask your spouse to clarify.

You may cringe at the thought of doing this kind of exercise, but if you try it, you'll be amazed at how it eases your relationship and reduces your partner's critical comments. Not only that, strange as it may sound, it also helps the Leader feel loved and respected.

Understand the Critical Gender Difference

Are there notable differences between men and women when it comes to loving a Take-Charge Spouse? Of course—but especially if you are a man who is trying to love a Take-Charge wife. In fact, this particular gender difference is so glaring for the husband of a wife with this Love Style that it demands a special note of attention.

Women, it seems, get labeled "nags" far more often than men. But according to Deborah Tannen, author of the bestselling book *You Just Don't Understand: Women and Men in Conversation*, that may be due to the different ways men and women have been raised.[10]

Women, compared to men, are brought up to please others, and to equate fulfilling requests with showing love (that's why this issue is not as important for the woman married to a Take-Charge husband). Men, on the other hand, equate receiving requests with taking orders and react accordingly: "Stop telling me what to do!" Consequently, when a husband fails to do what his wife asks, she feels hurt or puzzled, so she asks again. And again. And if she is a Take-Charge wife, she may unknowingly do this with all the subtlety of a drill sergeant. After all, she doesn't want time to be wasted.

But each time she reminds him, he feels less inclined to oblige. He'll then wait before doing what's requested so that he does it of his own free will—and not because he's been told to. Regardless of your gender—but especially if you are a woman who is a Take-Charge Spouse—it's helpful to remember this fundamental gender difference: Men want to fulfill a request on their own terms. That means you'll often get quicker results from them if you give them time to do just that.

And if you are a husband married to a Take-Charge wife, keep in mind that this gender difference applies to nearly every marriage—but it gets amped up a bit more in yours. Your wife's urgency meter as a Leader Spouse makes her perceived "ordering around" come off as especially sharp on occasion. Do your best to bite your tongue when you can and not take it personally. Once the task is done, she'll relax almost immediately and you will have avoided an unnecessary squabble.

Praise Liberally

The Leader Love Style deeply values appreciation and recognition. Your spouse loves to be honored, celebrated, and praised. It opens up your partner's spirit. It makes your spouse come alive—even if it doesn't immediately look like it. We're not talking about an official ceremony of adulation. We're talking about the little things you can say to communicate that your spouse is valued, respected, and loved. Here are a few examples:

"I want you to know that I really value what you do for our family."

"You are one of the most disciplined people I know."

"I don't know what I would do without you."

To make your praise even more powerful, get specific with your comments. You can say something like: "I overheard you talking with Jacob tonight, and I want you to know that you're a brilliant father." A concrete and specific compliment like this is sure to warm the heart of your Take-Charge Spouse. And the more often you do it—as long as you are genuine—the more you will feel the love in your marriage grow.

> Your Take-Charge Spouse Feels Most Loved …
> When you help him or her reach
> goals more efficiently.

How to Stay Healthy with a Take-Charge Spouse

One of the most important things you will ever do for your marriage is to stay healthy and strong yourself. If you don't take care of yourself, your marriage will suffer. So here are a few practical ways to stay healthy when married to a spouse with a Leader Love Style.

Don't Take It Personally

Remember that, in most cases, Take-Charge Spouses are trying to protect themselves; they are not trying to hurt you. Don't feel responsible or try to make things better when they get upset. Accusing them of being controlling will only make them more fearful and controlling. Instead, tell them how the behavior makes you feel. This made a big difference for me (Leslie) in our marriage when I figured out how to respond to Les without taking it personally. For example, you might say, "You may not be aware of this, but whenever we get together, it seems that we end up doing things your way. This is very frustrating for me. I'd like to start taking turns deciding on the restaurant or the movie." Expressing feelings is far better than making an accusation, like, "You never trust me with any decisions!" After all, the Leader's behavior really isn't about you; it's about how to avoid the anxiety of losing control. So don't take it personally.

When You Lose (and You Will), Do It with Dignity

Invariably, because you live with a Leader, you will lose something—your influence, your position, an argument, or your desires. But you don't have to lose your dignity. You may not get to choose the color of the new carpet in your bedroom, for example, or where you go on your next vacation, or the temperature on the thermostat. Losing some of your influence is a given when it comes to living with a Take-Charge Spouse.

But when those times occur, you can "lose" in the right way. For starters, you shouldn't expect to get in the last word. The Leader experiences this as a challenge and will prolong your agony. Instead, allow the Leader to have the last word—but do so on *your* terms. Say something like, "I am ready and willing to hear your decision, but only when you patiently walk me through your reasoning—and when you listen to mine." This kind of statement may mean that you give up the battle, but you win back your dignity.

> To behave with dignity is nothing less than to allow others to freely be themselves.
>
> *Sol Chaneles*

Set Your Boundaries

"This above all," said Shakespeare, "to thine own self be true." It was his Elizabethan way of saying to build some boundaries for yourself. Because you're married to a Take-Charge Spouse, you no doubt find yourself debating the same issues over and over: how you drive the car, the way dinner is prepared, and so on. When you identify a boomerang issue like this, call a marital meeting. Build a boundary.

Talk about who is best at certain tasks and who should control them. If you are a better cook, you should be in control of the kitchen, and the Leader needs to agree to stay clear. If he or she is better behind the wheel, he or she should drive the car. The trick to making this strategy work is to remind the Leader of your agreement. If your spouse starts telling you how to cut carrots, for example, say, "We agreed that this is my domain, and I am in control here." Maybe such delegated roles seem too formal and prescribed for you. They *can* be. But negotiating your pre-assigned roles can help you set healthy boundaries and ease your life with a Take-Charge Spouse.

You can also build a boundary whenever your spouse attempts to cut you down to size. If your partner is hurling insults, call a time-out. Call a penalty. Say something like, "That comment is out of bounds, and I do not deserve to be spoken to like that." In other words, build a boundary that protects you from being bossed around by a bully.

Tame Your Inner Gremlin

Let's take boundary setting one step further. We all have "soft spots," areas that are particularly vulnerable and sensitive. When your spouse approaches one of those areas with a critical comment, you're likely to hear another critical voice—this one from within your own head—and absorb extra emotional pain. You may say, for example, *He's right, I am inept.* Or, *I'll never be good at this.* Of course, you already know this is not healthy. So how can you keep from doing it?

Family therapist Richard Carson identifies that inner narrator who puts you down and tries to convince you that whatever critical comments you hear are true. Carson calls that voice our internal "gremlin." Gremlins are troublesome creatures bent on sabotage. The gremlin in your head is quick to jump on the bandwagon of your spouse's critical parade. But don't you let it.

> I know myself now; and I feel within me a peace above all earthly dignities, a still and quiet conscience.
>
> *William Shakespeare*

Keep your internal gremlin from wreaking havoc by guarding your soft spots carefully from your spouse. Declare them off-limits, and make no bones about it. Say,

"You can evaluate or critique anything I do, but don't tell me how to handle the relationship with my sister. For right now, that is my business, not yours." Or, "I can handle your critical comments most of the time, but not about my weight. That's not an area you can critique." This is the surest way to tame your inner gremlin.

For Reflection and Discussion

1. What is it like being married to a spouse with this Love Style? In other words, what are the benefits and what are the challenges of living with this particular style? Be specific.

2. Now that you have a clearer understanding of what makes your spouse feel most loved, what is one thing you can do in the next day or so to do just that? Which of the suggestions in this chapter seem most challenging to you when it comes to loving your spouse? Why?

3. When it comes to staying healthy with your spouse's Love Style, which suggestion in this chapter do you personally feel could benefit you the most? How, in specific terms, can you begin putting it into practice?

WORKBOOK EXERCISE
for the Spouse of a Leader

If you're electing to use the optional his/her interactive workbooks, you'll want to turn to the exercise designed specifically for you to apply this chapter to your marriage. It contains several brief exercises that are sure to make this information come alive in your relationship.

IF YOU'RE MARRIED TO AN OPTIMIST

Love me when I least deserve it,
because that's when I really need it.

Swedish Proverb

SOMEBODY SAID THAT, "A pessimist is an optimist with experience." Maybe. But if optimists are merely less-experienced pessimists, if they are people who have their heads in the clouds and look at life through rose-colored glasses, well, it seems to be paying off.

A recent study of one thousand people underscores the value of optimism. After almost ten years of follow-up, researchers found that people who described themselves as optimistic had a fifty-five percent lower risk of death from all causes and a twenty-three percent lower risk of heart-related death. Optimistic people tend to be more physically active, drink less, and smoke less. They cope with stress more effectively.[11]

Not bad, right? But if you're married to a person with an Optimist Love Style, you may not agree that it's always rosy. Even the Encouraging Spouse presents some challenges. That's why we dedicate this chapter to giving you the most proven and effective strategies for making your relationship with an Optimist Spouse the very best it can be.

This chapter reveals exactly what you can expect from your spouse, what your spouse fears most, and what you need to do—in specific terms—to love your partner successfully. Finally, we show you how you can stay strong and healthy when married to an Encouraging Spouse.

What You Can Expect from an Optimist: The Encouraging Spouse

Let's cut straight to it. You can expect a lot of fun with a spouse who has an Optimist Love Style. Life with your spouse is exciting, spontaneous, surprising, adventurous, and filled with activity. You will never be bored. Exhausted? Maybe. But not bored.

Your spouse's fun-loving demeanor brings laughter and playfulness to your home. And you can probably expect a few practical jokes or big surprises, too. Your spouse lightens the mood and can make you feel better when nobody else can.

> Two men looked out of the prison bars and one saw mud and the other saw stars.
>
> *Anonymous*

Your partner seems to know just what to say to lift you up and keep you going. You're a more confident person because of your spouse (and the Encouraging Spouse loves to hear you acknowledge that).

You can also expect never to run low on friends. Because of your spouse, you have a warm and welcoming home. People are drawn to you as a couple because people like your spouse. They like you too, but make no mistake, you're more popular because of the person you married.

On the downside, when your spouse is at his or her worst, you can expect a fair amount of drama. That is, you'll find that little things can become big things when your spouse is not feeling particularly safe and accepted by you. A seemingly innocent comment you make, with just a tinge of bite to it, can turn into a marriage "issue," because your spouse reads more into it than you ever intended. If the issue isn't resolved quickly, then you can expect some serious pouting and sulking, or even complete withdrawal. That withdrawal, by the way, is just your spouse's way of saying, "Please pursue me." It's not a desire to punish you. Quite the opposite. In those tough times, your spouse wants you to follow up and make it right with a heavy dose of love.

> We come to love not by finding a perfect person, but by learning to see an imperfect person perfectly.
>
> *Sam Keen*

You can also expect some procrastination and forgetfulness. You may even be tempted to describe it as "passive-aggressive," and you'd be right. You see, your spouse is conflict-avoidant and the only way to get back at you without stirring up a real fight is to conveniently forget something or misplace something that matters to you. Of course, you can never quite pin aggression onto a passive act like this, so don't always assume that's the case. Just be aware that forgetfulness and procrastination are experiences that come with the package of an Encouraging Spouse.

Never lose sight of the fact that when your spouse's needs are being met, when he or she is feeling deeply accepted and loved by you, you can expect to have one of the most affectionate, supportive, energizing, fun, and active partners on the planet.

What Your Spouse Wants Most from You

- ♥ A loving and listening ear
- ♥ Sincere compliments
- ♥ Laughter and fun
- ♥ Room to be spontaneous (not pinned down)
- ♥ A chance to speak
- ♥ Unconditional acceptance

What Your Encouraging Spouse Fears Most

Pulitzer prize-winning journalist Henry Bayard Swope once noted, "I cannot give you the formula for success, but I can give you the formula for failure: Try to please everybody." Your Optimist Spouse, unfortunately, often tries to do just that. Does it lead to failure, as Swope says? Not necessarily. But it gets at your partner's deepest fear, and a big part of it is a fear of failing you.

Lisa and Steve, married fourteen years and deeply in love, still run into little glitches that cause Lisa's spirit to wilt. Lisa, an Encouraging Spouse, will notice if Steve doesn't eat as much as he normally does at dinner. Then she assumes it's because of her cooking. "You don't like your food, do you?" she'll ask. If Steve can't find the shirt he's looking for, Lisa scurries around to find it. "Maybe it's in the laundry room," she'll say. "I'll find it." If Steve comments on someone being on a diet, Lisa assumes he wants her to lose weight. It seems that almost every interaction, for Lisa, goes through a filter of poten-

> I've learned that people will forget what you said, people will forget what you did, but people will never forget how you made them feel.
>
> *Maya Angelou*

tial failure. That is, Lisa is tuned into potential signals that she's failing Steve, that she's losing his approval.

The need to please is at the core of the Encouraging Spouse's identity—and it comes from a fear of rejection. They dress to please, talk to please, behave to please, and smile no matter what. They are terrified by the slightest possibility of being snubbed or getting their feelings hurt by you. Approachable and ever-agreeable, your Encouraging Spouse is highly skilled at winning your approval. But if you're especially hard to win over, your spouse will try that much harder. Like the desert craves the rain, your spouse craves your approval—and desperately fears losing it.

Approval craving might seem like a strong term, but only a powerful word such as *craving* adequately describes the commanding hold this need has on your spouse. He or she lives in fear of your rejection.

How to Love an Encouraging Spouse

Everybody wants a happy marriage. And a happy marriage is the result of two people operating at the top of their game—where both spouses are functioning at their best, with the strengths from their inborn personalities in full play. With this in mind, here are a few specifics that will help you insure that your spouse can operate from the positive aspects of his or her God-given personality traits. It will also help you honor your spouse's Love Style.

Affirm Liberally

If you haven't got the message by now, let's make this crystal clear: Your spouse longs to be loved by you. He or she fears losing that love. If you want a happy home, if you're looking for a way to love your Encouraging Spouse, you can never go wrong with affirmation. Your spouse eats it up with a spoon.

The word *affirm*, in the Old French, literally means *to strengthen*. And the Latin stem of *dicere* means *to speak*.

> It gives me great pleasure indeed to see the stubbornness of an incorrigible nonconformist warmly acclaimed.
>
> *Albert Einstein*

Thus, to affirm your spouse means to say something that will make your partner stronger. This can be as simple as complimenting appearance or as profound as noting a wise parenting intervention. For example, "Earlier today I watched how you diffused the conflict brewing with the kids. I just want you to know that you did a great job—you're really an outstanding parent." Words like this make your spouse come alive, as long as you are genuine. Your affirmations have to come from the heart.

The point is that your spouse loves to be affirmed. So don't hold back, even if it's only a small affirmation that registers in your mind. Speak it out loud. It's one of the best ways to meet your spouse's deepest needs.

Be More Spontaneous

Your spouse loves spontaneous fun. If that's not part of your style, if you like to be more deliberate and planned out, you

> Conform and be dull.
>
> *J. Frank Doble*

can improve your relationship by giving in to the spontaneity from time to time. Even if it seems a bit crazy, don't make your spouse beg you to join in on the adventure. If that means hopping onto a water slide at an amusement park, do it. If it means blowing off yard work to enjoy a picnic lunch, do it.

Carl Sandburg once said, "Nearly all the best things that came to me in life have been unexpected and unplanned." You might find the same to be true for you when you go along with your spouse's whims. Embrace your Encouraging Spouse's need for excitement when you can. Your partner's lively spirit will lead you into many memorable experiences together. Joining in the fun is a sure way to say "I love you" to an Encouraging Spouse.

Share the Troubles

One of the easiest ways to shut down your spouse is to try and solve your partner's problem before you even understand it. Men often get a bad rap on this, and sometimes for good reason. But it can go both ways. Here's the key: When your spouse is sharing troubles, bite your tongue. Just listen. Be as patient as you can. Admittedly, your spouse can talk, but do your best not to interrupt. Maintain eye contact, and allow your partner to let the feelings flow.

> There is no more lovely, friendly and charming relationship, communion or company than a good marriage.
>
> *Martin Luther*

Once you've done this, then, and only then, should you try to hint around at potential solutions to the trouble. Even better, don't offer a solution unless your spouse specifically asks you for one. Just spend your time entering into your partner's feelings. Listen with compassion and understanding. Your spouse wants your sympathy when dealing with something tough. It's your sympathetic ear that will refuel the Optimistic Spouse's batteries and give a renewed sense of energy to face troubles again.

This may not feel like love to you, but we promise that it does to your Encouraging Spouse.

Clarify Their Details

Because your Optimist Spouse tends to exaggerate the good or overlook the bad, you can save yourself and your spouse some anguish by lovingly asking for the details. For example, when an Optimist Husband says he will be home in fifteen minutes and you suspect that's impossible with traffic, clarify, "Don't you think it will be more like thirty minutes this time of day?" This gives your Optimist Spouse the opportunity to face the facts instead of focusing entirely on your feelings. It gives the Optimist the chance to say something like, "You are probably right; it will be closer to thirty minutes."

A simple clarification opens a small window for your Encouraging Spouse to be more accurate with you. It may seem silly to you to have to clarify such small things, but remember that Optimists are peacemakers that will always try to put the best spin on their scenarios—to the point that they will deny or ignore that anything is ever wrong or late or difficult if they can avoid it. They are more concerned about peace and harmony with you than about blatant honesty. If you aren't doing so already, do yourself a favor and lovingly clarify your Optimist's details.

Ask for Honesty

"Say what you have to say, not what you ought," said Henry David Thoreau. That's hard advice for an Encouraging Spouse to swallow. And it can be extremely frustrating when a spouse, looking for an honest opinion, is married to an Optimist. Why? Because an Optimist doesn't like to hurt feelings—so the Encouraging Spouse has a tough time delivering bad news. Even if Optimists don't like something, they'll often put a positive spin on it.

Say you wallpaper the bathroom as a surprise for your spouse. "Wow! You really worked hard on this," they may say to you.

You press for details, "Yes, but what do you think? Now that it's up, I'm not sure it works."

"It's lovely," your spouse affirms, but you suspect he or she feels differently. You really want your spouse to weigh in honestly, but all you're getting are complimentary platitudes. What can you do? Remember, the last thing your spouse wants to do is offend you. That's why you'll need to give a little nudge. Many times, a straightforward request for an honest opinion is all that is required: "I really want to know what you're thinking; I want your honest feedback." An invitation to be honest, to speak one's mind, is what the Optimist needs to open up with any kind of negativity related to your work. Make it clear that your partner's opinion and even criticism won't offend you.

> Be who you are and say what you feel because those who mind don't matter and those who matter don't mind.
>
> *Dr. Seuss*

For example, instead of saying, "What do you think about this letter I wrote?" say, "If you were me, what would you change about this letter? I really need some honest and objective input." Even then you may have to keep prodding. But the more often you invite your Optimist Spouse to speak plainly, the more honesty you'll receive. More importantly, inviting direct feedback helps your spouse to see that being

> We hardly find any persons of good sense save those who agree with us.
>
> *François de La Rochefoucauld*

honest with negative information is not as frightening as your partner thought. It helps your spouse become more balanced. And that's always a loving expression.

Show More Affection

If your spouse were an automobile, he or she would run on affection. Affection fuels loving feelings for anyone with an Optimist Love Style. And it's so easy to express. It can be verbal or nonverbal. You have a million opportunities everyday to express your fondness, that you have tender, warmhearted feelings for them. You can use a gentle caress, a loving wink, a turned-down bedside, or any other gesture of kindness and caring.

> To hope is to risk frustration.
>
> *Thomas Merton*

Jack never really understood the value of expressing affection to his Encouraging Spouse until he attended one of our seminars. A few weeks later, he sent us an email: "I thought I'd give it a try. So I stopped by her office yesterday with her favorite coffee drink, and I asked the receptionist to bring it to her as a little surprise. I wrote 'Glad you're mine' on the lid. That was it. Well, you would have thought I gave her a trip to Hawaii. She called me on the phone that afternoon and was gushing. And that evening, well, it was fantastic!"

Jack became a believer. You will be too when you experiment with a few acts of warm affection for your Encouraging Spouse.

Flex on the Schedule

Do you remember the rabbit in Alice's Wonderland? He frantically rushed around from place to place, always excusing himself with, "I'm late! I'm late, for a very important date!"

Chances are, on occasion, you've felt like you were married to that rabbit. While most spouses with an Optimist Love Style are endlessly busy, many are also desperate not to be late because they know it can create friction. Being chronically late can make it tough to maintain the peace. When an Optimist is late, there's usually a legitimate reason. Of course, it could also be that the Encouraging Spouse simply could not leave an enjoyable conversation, even knowing it would cause tardiness for the next appointment.

Whatever the reason, legitimate or not, you can be a more loving spouse by learning to flex a bit more with your spouse's sometimes-surprising schedule. In practical terms, this means saying things like, "We're all late sometimes. I understand." Or, if you're not feeling that generous, "I know you've been rushing to get here. Next time I'd just like you to respect my schedule, too." That's far better than saying, "You're so disrespectful—I can't believe you did this!" A negative comment like this crushes your partner's spirit. Be as flexible and gentle as you can without continually sacrificing your own scheduling needs.

Your Encouraging Spouse Feels Most Loved…
When your relationship is filled with
expressions of affirmation and affection.

How to Stay Healthy with an Encouraging Spouse

One of the most important things you will ever do for your marriage is to stay healthy and strong yourself. If you don't take care of yourself, your marriage will suffer. So here are a few practical ways of doing just that—when married to an Optimist.

Take a Break When Needed

Living with an Encouraging Spouse has a lot of advantages. But sometimes the whirlwind of activity and the fully booked social schedule can grow wearisome if you aren't wired in a similar way. If that's the case for you, we recommend you find some practical ways of letting your own spirit catch

> It is better to be hated for what you are than loved for what you are not.
>
> *André Gide*

up. In other words, we suggest you hit the brakes when and if you need to so you maintain your own sense of well-being.

An Optimist Spouse has the potential to run some Love Styles ragged. It's typically not the Take-Charge Spouse (they won't stand for it), but it may be the spouse with a Validator Love Style or Evaluator Love Style. If that's you, consider where and when you need to take a rest. Talk to your spouse about it in a loving way. You can say something like, "I love the energy and the adventures you bring to our marriage, but I'm not wired the same way. I sometimes need a moment to catch my breath." From there, describe what would help you do just that. It may mean a nap on Sunday afternoons. It may mean an escape to your den or study for some uninterrupted time you can count on.

The point is that you need to protect your own spirit so that it does not become overpowered and continually depleted by your partner's energy and social activity.

Set Your Boundaries

Every healthy marriage has boundary lines that protect each spouse from getting hurt. If you haven't already established yours with your spouse, you need to. Boundaries are nothing more than what you are willing to say *yes* to and what you are sure to say *no* to.

Earlier in this chapter, we encouraged you to love your spouse better by being more spontaneous—especially if you live by a rigid schedule. But don't take this to mean that you should never say no to a spontaneous request from your spouse. If you're feeling particular pressure from your spouse about doing that, we want to encourage you to set a boundary that your spouse knows about.

For example, you may be willing to drop what you're doing and go to an amusement park with friends. But if you have a fear of roller coasters, by all means you don't need to cave in to pressure from your spouse to ride one. That, for you, may be crossing a boundary you'd like to keep. Once your partner understands how much this matters to you, your spouse should respect it. Of course, boundaries can be set around anything and everything that makes you feel especially anxious. They can also be set around anything that drains you of energy. For example, you might be willing to attend a party with your spouse, but not stay longer than two hours.

Set some boundaries that protect your needs. Your marriage will be the better for it.

Undo Any "Unmet" Needs

Because your spouse is so often eager to meet your needs and win your approval, your Optimist may be meeting needs that you don't have. Your spouse, for example, may be under the mistaken impression that you love watching the nightly news, playing Scrabble, having your feet rubbed, or whatever. Somewhere along the way, especially if you are a Devoted Spouse, you may have given the impression that you really enjoyed something that, in fact, you never really did enjoy or that you no longer enjoy. And your Encouraging Spouse keeps meeting that need.

This isn't likely if you are a person with a Leader Love Style, but if something comes to mind, let your spouse know that the activity is not really something you enjoy, that it's not a need you really have. Of course, break this news gently. After all, your spouse is only doing this thinking mistakenly that it's a gift. Say something like, "You take such good care of me, but this is something you don't really need to meet for me." Your spouse may be surprised, but that's okay. No need for you to live with a need being met that you don't have.

> There is no conversation more boring than the one where everybody agrees.
>
> *Michel de Montaigne*

Direct the Drama

You already know your spouse can sometimes make a mountain out of the proverbial molehill. You've seen the occasions when your spouse exaggerates struggles and embellishes stories. And chances are that you've been sucked into these experiences for good reasons.

But over the years of marriage you may realize that you feel a little played. That is, you gave in a little too much to a dramatic episode that, in retrospect, didn't really require that much of your energy. It may have been a story about a reckless driver or a rude coworker or any number of "dramatic" incidents.

> Love is a fruit in season at all times, and within reach of every hand.
>
> *Mother Teresa*

That's okay. Feel free to get wrapped up in the drama of your spouse's stories. But if they sometimes deplete your energy or if they needlessly rile you, take a step back. Say to yourself, "This is interesting." That's all it takes. This little self-statement gives you a bit of objectivity. It helps you be an observer as well as a participant. It helps you direct the drama, as it were. And you can do so without distancing yourself from your spouse, as long as you continue to lend a loving and listening ear when needed.

For Reflection and Discussion

1. What is it like being married to a spouse with this Love Style? In other words, what are the benefits and what are the challenges of living with this particular style? Be specific.

2. Now that you have a clearer understanding of what makes your spouse feel most loved, what is one thing you can do in the next day or so to do just that? Which of the suggestions in this chapter seem most challenging to you when it comes to loving your spouse? Why?

3. When it comes to staying healthy with your spouse's Love Style, which suggestion in this chapter do you personally feel could benefit you the most? How, in specific terms, can you begin putting it into practice?

WORKBOOK EXERCISE
for the Spouse of an Optimist

If you're electing to use the optional his/her interactive workbooks, you'll want to turn to the exercise designed specifically for you to apply this chapter to your marriage. It contains several brief exercises that are sure to make this information come alive in your relationship.

IF YOU'RE MARRIED TO A VALIDATOR

Peace is always beautiful.

Walt Whitman

IF YOU LOOK up *validate* in the dictionary, it will tell you that it means to substantiate or confirm. That's just what your spouse is all about—but on a more personal level. We call your Devoted Spouse a Validator because your partner wants to have everyone's feelings and opinions validated. Your spouse wants that, and your Validator wants that for you as well. Why? Because it's the best way we humans have for maintaining peaceful relationships. And your spouse, above all, prizes peace.

In fact, your spouse is intricately designed to do whatever he or she can do to maintain peace in your marriage. That's why your partner consistently validates you by insuring that your feelings and opinions are acknowledged, respected, and heard. Regardless of whether or not your spouse actually agrees

> Few things are brought to a successful issue by impetuous desire, but most by calm and prudent forethought.
>
> *Thucydides*

with what you are saying, the Validator Spouse almost always treats you with genuine respect, taking care not to marginalize or dismiss your opinions or contributions.

This kind of validation is a gift that not everyone receives from a spouse. But it is so consistently offered to you that you may have begun to take it for granted. Of course, the strong desire for peace often comes with a price. You've no doubt noticed that your spouse brings other traits and qualities into your relationship that can either be helpful or detrimental to the kind of marriage you'd like to have. In other words, your spouse, like you and everyone else, presents a few challenges along with some wonderful gifts.

This chapter reveals exactly what you can expect from your spouse, what your spouse fears most, and what you need to do — in specific terms — to love your spouse successfully. Finally, we show you how you can stay strong and healthy when married to a Devoted Spouse.

What You Can Expect from a Validator: The Devoted Spouse

Your spouse has a stronger people-orientation than project-orientation. And your spouse is more slow-paced than fast-paced. This makes them feel most comfortable when life is moving at a steady rate with no sudden or unexpected changes. In fact, you can expect your spouse to be very slow in coming around to accept a change of almost any kind. It might be changing your dinner plans for the evening or changing something as significant as a job or career. Whatever the change, your spouse is likely to resist it, at least at the start. In time, the Devoted Spouse may come around to supporting it. But expect your partner to need plenty of time to do so.

You can also expect the Validator to finish anything started. When your spouse makes a commitment, it's as good as done. Your partner will persevere when others would likely give up or put it off. Not the Devoted Spouse. Your spouse will make every effort to follow through on promises. And your spouse wants you to do the same. If you don't, you can expect the Devoted Spouse to be upset. Your spouse will clam up, and if you are tuned in at all, you'll know you let your partner down.

> Be like a duck. Calm on the surface, but always paddling like the dickens underneath.
>
> *Michael Caine*

Speaking of clamming up, you can expect your spouse to be relatively quiet most of the time. You've no doubt experienced times in your marriage when you wondered what your spouse was really feeling. The Devoted Spouse's face doesn't seem to give it away, nor do your partner's words or vocal responses. If you're excited, don't count on your spouse joining in the celebration — at least to the extent that others might. In fact, your spouse sometimes seems just a bit distant and is likely an introvert. Your spouse may be engaged with you, but more as an observer than a participant.

You can expect your spouse to be very steadfast and loyal. It's one of the hallmarks of the Validator. Your partner will stand by you through thick and thin, for better or worse. In fact, you're married to the most loyal of Love Styles. As we mentioned, the Devoted Spouse doesn't readily embrace change of any kind, and that includes changing the devotion to you.

> There is no joy but calm.
>
> *Alfred, Lord Tennyson*

Keep in mind that when your spouse's needs are being met, when he or she is feeling at peace and life is stable, you can expect to have one of the most easygoing, peace-loving cheerful, thoughtful, dependable, and relaxed spouses on the planet.

What Your Spouse Wants Most from You

- ♥ A calm presence
- ♥ Courtesy and patience
- ♥ Unrushed time with you
- ♥ Advance warning of change
- ♥ Time to reflect
- ♥ Trust and meaning

What Your Devoted Spouse Fears Most

We can sum up the deepest fear of your spouse in a single word: Change. Your spouse loves a routine and a plan that can be counted on. The Devoted Spouse holds to it with tenacity. Even a small change is disconcerting to your spouse. If the waitress who usually brings your spouse coffee at his or her favorite cafe suddenly quits, your spouse feels out of balance. You can imagine the fear the Devoted Spouse harbors about changes you might impose on life.

If you simply bring up the idea that you are considering a career change or that your job might require relocating, it pushes the panic button in your spouse's spirit. Your partner won't freak out externally (that would cause conflict), but inside the Validator is suddenly in turmoil. You are likely to think of change as either exciting or inevitable. But your spouse thinks of change as avoidable—if you both simply follow the original plan.

Along with this fear of change comes a fear of losing security. That's what change represents to your Devoted

Spouse. Your spouse is so devoted to you, in fact, that change—positive or negative—feels like it could jeopardize your relationship. Your spouse would rather play it safe. Change is risky. Change means the possible loss of what you both have come to expect. It means being nudged out of a comfort zone. A career change, for example, might mean you have less time together or that your social circle would not be as pleasant. Change simply feels unsafe to your spouse.

> The true genius shudders at incompleteness—and usually prefers silence to saying something which is not everything it should be.
>
> *Edgar Allan Poe*

Of course, your spouse also fears conflict. Because peace is such a high priority, your Devoted Spouse will do everything possible to keep discord at bay. Conflict, like change, dismantles security. Conflict leads to unpredictable outcomes. Conflict, for your spouse, is scary. Your partner lives in fear of both disagreement and change, because these experiences render life inconsistent, erratic, and unpredictable. These shake your spouse to the core.

How to Love a Devoted Spouse

Everybody wants a happy marriage. And a happy marriage is the result of two people operating at the top of their game—where both spouses are functioning at their best, with the strengths from their inborn personalities in full play. With this in mind, here are a few specifics that will help you ensure that your spouse can operate from the positive aspects of his or her God-given personality traits. It will also help you honor your spouse's Love Style.

Cultivate Significance

Because your spouse works diligently to keep conflict from erupting and can come across as a bit aloof or detached in doing so, your partner has a special need for significance and inclusion. After all, staying out of trouble gets the Devoted Spouse less attention, both positive and negative, than most other people. And while being low-key and a bit ignored can make life peaceful, it can also instill feelings of insignificance.

Chances are that you are happy to include your spouse in decision-making and meaningful conversations that would contribute to a feeling of significance, but when you do, you often feel like your partner isn't participating. That's okay. It's still meaningful. Even if your spouse comes off as not caring, don't give up on this. That seeming lack of care is just external. Inside, your Devoted Spouse feels great about being brought into the conversation. If your spouse seems happy to let you make most of the decisions, there is still a desire to be included in the decision-making process. It's critically important that you make it easy for your partner to participate. One of the best ways to do this is to ask your spouse open-ended questions, not "yes" or "no" questions. For example, instead of saying, "Do you feel good about us making this investment?" say, "How do you feel about us making this investment?" Open-ended questions draw your spouse into the conversation.

By the way, make sure that you are especially careful not to interrupt your spouse when you're posing these questions. Your partner may not speak much, but when words are spoken, they are important. Treat them as

> Dreams are illustrations...from the book your soul is writing about you.
>
> *Marsha Norman*

such. This is all part of cultivating more significance for your partner. It's a wonderful way to love your Devoted Spouse.

Provide Warning of Change

You already know that your spouse resists change of any kind. Of course, change is inevitable. Life is unpredictable. However, you can make the changes you anticipate much easier for your spouse to handle by giving advance warning. Think of it like driving down a long stretch of road and spotting a sign that indicates the paved road will become a gravel road in a certain number of miles. The sign gives you time to prepare yourself. You get a mindset for what is about to happen. It makes for a smoother transition from one thing to the next. You do the same thing for your spouse when you give warning about a likely change coming down the road of your life.

If you believe that your vacation dates, for example, will likely need to be cut back this summer because of a major event at work, don't put off telling your Devoted Spouse about it. You can say something like, "I know you are counting on taking vacation in mid-June, but I just found out that my boss scheduled an important meeting that week. It may mean we'll have to cut our vacation short so I can be there." Then, follow up with, "This isn't certain. It's just a possibility, and I know that it can be helpful to know what's going on just in case we have to adapt our vacation plans a bit."

> God promises a safe landing but not a calm passage.
> *Bulgarian Proverb*

Something like this may initially cause consternation for your Devoted Spouse, but your partner would rather get the news now than later, when there's little time to adjust. You may be inclined to put off news like this until you know it is certain, but if the delay doesn't give your spouse adequate time to adjust, it's not worth it. Instead, give your spouse advance warning of possible change.

Provide Time for Adjustment

This goes along with giving your spouse a warning of change. Once a change has taken place, your spouse needs time to readjust. Think of your spouse as a thermostat. You can move the temperature up or down on the dial, but the room temperature doesn't change instantaneously. The same holds true for the Devoted Spouse, who needs time to adjust and find a new and peaceful resting place.

William, a Validator, knew that the change to a new neighborhood would be an adjustment. He'd been preparing for the move, just a few miles from their old home in the same town, for months—ever since he and his wife decided that it would be beneficial financially to make the change. It took him awhile to warm up to that decision, but he came around. Now that it's done, he needs more time to adjust to it than his wife. For example, William is unsettled about the new floor plan and doesn't like how their furniture is situated in the new place. He also mumbled something about the house being farther away from a grocery store. He seems to be spending an inordinate amount of time watching TV when the boxes still need to be unpacked.

William's wife thinks the move is exciting and fun. But William isn't adding anything to the celebration—at least not yet. After a couple of weeks, when he reset his "temperature" and finally warmed up to the move, he's back on board.

That's life with a Validator. You can save yourself and your marriage some undue stress by knowing what to expect. Instead of saying, "You said you were for this move. I don't understand why you're not happier about it," bite your tongue and allow your spouse a little more time to adjust.

By the way, this applies to smaller changes as well. If your plans for an evening out with friends suddenly fall through, expect your spouse to take the adjustment harder than you do—even if your spouse doesn't express it. Just know it will take a bit more time until the Validator is back in the groove with you.

Stay Calm

One of the most loving things you can do for a spouse with a Validator Love Style is to remain cool and calm when you're tempted to lose your composure. This is particularly true when you are frustrated with your spouse. Of course, this is easier said than done—especially if you are an expressive Leader or an Optimist. But here is one proven strategy that can help.

If you want to remain calm when your feathers are getting ruffled, keep in mind that whatever is irritating you is only temporary. Research shows that emotions escalate when we view our circumstances as permanent. Say, for example, you're discussing an important topic like what school your child

> Be calm in arguing; for fierceness makes error a fault, and truth discourtesy.
>
> *George Herbert*

should attend. You become frustrated because your spouse isn't saying much. It seems like he or she isn't involved with you and helping to make a decision. You're tempted to say something like, "What's wrong with you? Why aren't you talking? Do you have an opinion on this or not?" If you act on the assumption that your spouse will never, ever reveal true feelings — that it will always be like this — you're far more likely to erupt emotionally than if you assume that your spouse will eventually, in his or her own timing, talk to you about thoughts and feelings.

Abraham Lincoln is a great model for this. The Civil War caused him immense despair, sadness, and pain. To keep himself calm enough to deal with it and make wise decisions in the midst of very emotional circumstances, he often said to himself, *This too shall pass.* He used this phrase as a kind of mantra. He was able to maintain his rationality and calmly carry out his duties at a crucial time in history, largely by reminding himself again and again that most circumstances are temporary.

Give it a try. The next time you find yourself in a contentious conversation with your spouse, remind yourself that it is only temporary. Say to yourself, *This too shall pass.* It's sure to lower your frustration level and keep you calm. And your spouse will love you more for doing it.

Give Your Time

In the Broadway play *My Fair Lady*, Eliza is courted by a man named Freddy. Freddy writes her love letters every day. But Eliza's response to all of these written promises is to cry out in frustration: "Words! Words! I'm so sick of words! Don't talk of stars burning above! If you're in love, show me! Don't talk of love lasting through time. Make no undying vow. If you love me, show me now!"

> Love must be fed and nurtured...first and foremost it demands time.
>
> *David Mace*

On occasion, your Devoted Spouse feels a bit like Eliza. Your spouse may like to hear you say how much you love them, but the Validator really likes to have you spend time together. Now, if you're a person with a Leader Love Style, a person who is fast-paced, this can sometimes feel excruciating. After all, the kind of time your Devoted Spouse wants is not necessarily "productive" time. Your partner simplys want you to hang out and do nothing together. You don't even need to have a conversation.

Your Devoted Spouse would likely love it if you'd just watch a DVD or television together. Or even be in the same room reading books. Lingering in the kitchen while a meal is prepared is good, or just sitting on a chair nearby while your spouse is working in the garden. The activity is not the main thing. The conversation is not even critical. It's that you are present with your spouse.

If you want to better love your Devoted Spouse, then give your partner as much of your time as you can.

Don't Push or Pressure

Have you ever seen your Devoted Spouse freeze up and become immobile? Maybe you're running errands and trying to do so at a quick clip in order to make some dinner reservations across town. You urge your spouse to pick up a prescription at the drugstore while you circle the block because you can't find a parking place. "Just jump out and go straight to the counter. I'll meet you on the opposite side of the street to avoid the light going the other way when I come around."

"What?" your Validator calmly asks.

"Just go. I can't stay here much longer," you snap.

But your spouse just sits there in the passenger seat, almost in a daze. You're wondering what's going on. It looks like your spouse is suffering brain lock. You speak more sharply: "Are you going to do this or not?"

Well, the reason your Devoted Spouse has become immobile is because you've gotten too pushy. If you want your spouse to get moving, you've got to stop shouting.

Yelling produces paralysis in your partner. The Validator doesn't respond well to pressure. In fact, your partner tends to shut down around it.

If you want to motivate your Devoted Spouse, then you need to coax with kindness. Say something like, "Since we can't find a parking space, how do you feel about me letting you off up here to pick up the prescription while I circle in the car?"

> I never undertake any more work than I can go through with perfect calmness of spirit.
>
> *John Wesley*

Your spouse will respond just fine to this approach. It doesn't sound as urgent, as loud, or as pressure-packed. And that makes all the difference. Coaxing with kindness is one of the most practical ways you'll find of loving your Devoted Spouse.

Recognize Your Spouse's Contribution

Your spouse's strengths are often overlooked. They are so much a part of the foundation that helps you have a happy marriage that you'll simply take them for granted. This adds to your partner's need to feel more significant in the marriage, and it makes for a wonderful opportunity to show them more love.

Here's what we recommend. Make a list of a few recent contributions your spouse has made to your marriage. Things you are grateful for. Maybe it's maintaining a peaceful home life. Maybe it's being so consistently nurturing with your child. Maybe it's helping you on a project. Write down whatever comes to mind. Just make sure you have a specific example and that it's recent, within the past few days.

Next, choose one of the items you listed and write a note to your Devoted Spouse. Express your heartfelt appreciation for that contribution to the relationship. You may want to express how you too often take this contribution for granted. The point of the note is simply to let your spouse know how much you value this important contribution. Of course, it doesn't need to be a note. It could be something you tell your spouse. But if

> He who seldom speaks, and with one calm well-timed word can strike dumb the loquacious, is a genius or a hero.
>
> *Johann Kaspar Lavater*

you take the time to write it out, your spouse is sure to treasure it and read it again in the days that follow.

If it's been awhile since you've expressed this kind of specific and sincere appreciation for your partner, why not do so sometime soon? Your Devoted Spouse will love it.

Your Devoted Spouse Feels Most Loved ...
When your relationship feels secure and stable.

How to Stay Healthy with a Devoted Spouse

One of the most important things you will ever do for your marriage is to stay healthy and strong yourself. If you don't take care of yourself, your marriage will suffer. So here are a few practical ways of doing just that—when married to a Validator.

Find an Outlet for Frustration

You already know that your Devoted Spouse can't stomach conflict. You know that the mere thought of a quarrel makes your partner anxious. The Devoted Spouse gives in and surrenders quickly—at least on the surface—so the tension passes. But that's probably not satisfying to you. If you're having a genuine difference of opinion, you probably want to hash it out. If that's not going to happen with your spouse, find a constructive outlet for your frustrations. This will help you get closure on your unfinished feelings.

How can you do this? That depends on you and your personality. If you are an Evaluator, for example, you may find it helpful to journal your thoughts and feelings about the disagreement. You can vent freely on a piece of paper

> Vows made in storms are forgotten in calm.
>
> *Thomas Fuller*

that nobody but you ever reads. If you are a Leader, you may find it more constructive to go to the gym and work out your frustrations with exercise or by jogging. If you are an Optimist, it may mean talking out your frustrations with a trusted friend (as long as your spouse approves). You get the idea. The point is to find a way that you can get some closure to frustration when your spouse is apt to quickly concede and leave you with unsatisfying emotional loose ends.

Don't Take Pessimism Personally

Because your spouse is not as exuberant and expressive as some, you may be tempted to read more pessimism into his or her communication than is intended. You wonder why your Devoted Spouse doesn't express more excitement about a new idea you have. Since your spouse stays so calm when you describe it, you assume your partner isn't for it. Whether that's true or not, it's not very encouraging to have a spouse who comes off as subdued when you're excited.

Maybe you have an idea about remodeling the kitchen. You've just seen a television program that inspires you.

"What if we pushed out this wall four feet and made a little bigger eating area here?" you ask in a fun and spontaneous way. Your spouse just looks at you blankly, waits for a moment, then says, "I like it just the way it is." Ouch! You feel shot down and a bit wounded.

As best you can, don't take it personally. Truth be told, your Devoted Spouse may love your idea but is literally hardwired to hold in excitement for a variety of reasons. It's understandable that you would feel let down. Just don't let it keep you down. In fact, you can try to laugh about it, if your spouse is receptive. "I knew you'd love the idea," you can say with a smile and a kiss. Your spouse may eventually express positive feelings. But in the meantime, find some ways to keep the initial pessimism from getting under your skin. It's not about you or your idea. It's about your Devoted Spouse's need for time to warm up to it.

Find a Critic

This may sound a bit strange, but because your spouse is so willing to get along and not make waves, you may find it helpful to cultivate a relationship where you know you'll get honest feedback. Of course, nobody really wants someone to come in for the sole purpose of criticizing. That's not what we're talking about.

We're talking about a friend or

> It is only the cynicism that is born of success that is penetrating and valid.
>
> *George Jean Nathan*

a colleague who will give you honest feedback and critiques on ideas or projects when your spouse won't. For example, you may have some insecurity about your wardrobe and keeping it up-to-date. You wonder if a few things in your closet need to be eliminated. But when you ask your Devoted Spouse for an opinion you simply hear, "I think that looks nice on you." Your spouse is not going to say anything that runs the risk of hurting your feelings or causing difficulty in the relationship. What you need is an honest-to-goodness critic. You need someone who won't hold back.

So rather than try to pressure your spouse into that uncomfortable role, and rather than being frustrated that your partner won't do it, simply seek out a "critical" friend who will shoot straight when that's what you want.

Allow Yourself to Dream

Chances are that you may have shut down some of your spontaneous dreaming because your spouse is reluctant to join in. After all, if you were designed to resist change, your favorite pastime would not be dreaming about what might be in the future. Dreams, by their very nature, involve change.

> You are never too old to set another goal or to dream a new dream.
>
> *C. S. Lewis*

Dreams, if they stick, engender goals. And goals create pressure. That's something your spouse isn't particularly fond of.

If you're a dreamer who has stifled your dreams, don't give up. You need to release your inner inspirations in a way that doesn't threaten your Devoted Spouse's need for stability.

You might find it helpful to keep a dream journal, a place where you can freely write about what could be. If this isn't your inclination, attend an event (and include your spouse, if willing) that you think will inspire you. It could be anything from a writing workshop to a motivational seminar. Or find a friend who is willing to talk about aspirations and visions for the future. Of course, you won't want to keep this from your spouse. You can be straight up about what you are doing and why. Just do so in a compassionate way that helps your partner understand why this need is important to you.

For Reflection and Discussion

1. What is it like being married to a spouse with this Love Style? In other words, what are the benefits and what are the challenges of living with this particular style? Be specific.

2. Now that you have a clearer understanding of what makes your spouse feel most loved, what is one thing you can do in the next day or so to do just that? Which of the suggestions in this chapter seem most challenging to you when it comes to loving your spouse? Why?

3. When it comes to staying healthy with your spouse's Love Style, which suggestion in this chapter do you personally feel could benefit you the most? How, in specific terms, can you begin putting it into practice?

WORKBOOK EXERCISE
for the Spouse of a Validator

If you're electing to use the optional his/her interactive workbooks, you'll want to turn to the exercise designed specifically for you to apply this chapter to your marriage. It contains several brief exercises that are sure to make this information come alive in your relationship.

IF YOU'RE MARRIED TO AN EVALUATOR

Be of love more careful than of anything.

E. E. Cummings

MARCUS FOUND AN innovative gadget for neatly dispensing toothpaste—a gadget only a Careful Spouse could truly love. Once installed on the bathroom wall, the sleek aluminum canister gently dispensed just the right amount of paste on his toothbrush. All he had to do was push the bristled end of his toothbrush into the hole at the bottom of the canister. The shiny gadget concealed the eventually disfigured tube inside as it consistently emptied its contents day after day.

"Isn't this terrific?" Marcus said to his wife. "You don't have to look at the toothpaste tube anymore. There's no messy cap, and there's no wasted paste. It's perfect!"

That's what your Evaluator Spouse longs for, not necessarily the latest in toothpaste dispensers, but "perfection." Whatever the endeavor, the person with an Evaluative Love Style is looking for quality, flawlessness, and excellence.

The dictionary defines *evaluate* as a verb meaning to "judge the quality of." You may be asking: *of what?* The Answer: *You name it*. The Careful Spouse judges the quality of *everything*—including you. Your spouse is hardwired to carefully evaluate anything and everything. As with every Love Style, the Evaluator brings both blessings and challenges to the relationship.

This chapter reveals exactly what you can expect from your Evaluator Spouse, what your spouse fears most, and what you need to do—in specific terms—to love your spouse successfully. Finally, we show you how you can stay strong and healthy when married to a Careful Spouse.

What You Can Expect from the Evaluator: The Careful Spouse

You're married to an introverted, logical, and analytical person. Your spouse, more than most people, is factual, neat, and precise. Your partner is a let's-do-it-right person. So you can expect to have some pretty-high standards around your home. In fact, doing everything the right way is one of your Careful Spouse's deepest needs. Your spouse doesn't just do online research about the best camera to buy at the best price. No, your partner also reads the owner's manual front-to-back once the camera is purchased. The Careful Spouse wants all the facts and details so you can take the best photos possible. A person with an Evaluative Love Style won't settle for anything that's middle-of-the-road or substandard. It's not an exaggeration to say the goal is perfection.

The word *evaluate* also means to assess and to appraise, and this is exactly what your spouse does in your marriage. The Careful Spouse reviews and appraises how things are done and "suggests" ways of improving them. Of course, these suggestions can be more than subtle. Because your spouse is more Project-Oriented than People-Oriented, the suggestions can be downright critical and aggressive at times.

"It's like my husband can't keep from criticizing me," the wife of a Careful Spouse confessed. "For example, the kids' meals. He thinks they should have two vegetables at every meal. Okay. So I make sure that happens. But then he comes up with something else, like he thinks the kids go to bed later than they should. Sometimes he makes me feel like a terrible parent—when I know I'm not." Evaluators have a way of doing that. They sit on a self-designed throne, pass laws, and pronounce verdicts.

At other times, your spouse responds to you in a slow, cautious, and sometimes indirect manner—especially when unsure of your intentions. You may simply want to know about your spouse's lunch with a friend, but your partner thinks you might have a hidden agenda behind the question. So the Careful Spouse comes off as reserved and even suspicious until the reason you are asking is confirmed.

> Try as hard as we may for perfection, the net result of our labors is an amazing variety of imperfections.
>
> *Samuel McChord Crothers*

You can expect your spouse to be sensitive to what others think—and especially sensitive to your opinions and evaluations. A negative comment from you can send the Evaluator into a moody funk.

If you are somewhat impatient, you can expect to have your patience tested when your spouse is making a decision. Why? Because your Careful Spouse is determined to make the right and best decision, agonizing over it. But once his mind is made up, you'll have a tough time changing it.

In spite of some of these more challenging characteristics, your spouse can be one of the most quality persons you'll ever find. The Careful Spouse not only wants the best in whatever is done, but also your partner wants the best for you and your marriage.

What Your Spouse Wants Most from You

- ♥ Lots of clear, detailed information
- ♥ Respect for his space
- ♥ Time to do things right
- ♥ Appreciation of efforts
- ♥ Time to think
- ♥ Justification of any deviation from the norm

What Your Careful Spouse Fears Most

One of the biggest fears your partner has is of making a mistake. Because the Careful Spouse is so meticulous about nearly every detail, your partner works diligently to be sure nothing is left to chance. The Evaluator covers all the bases, thinks through scenarios, sometimes even obsesses or worries about outcomes. That's why a mistake in your spouse's world is so dreadful. It points to a perceived sense of failure for the Careful Spouse that feels nearly unbearable. The Evaluator's self-worth rides on being competent and effective. A single mistake, in your spouse's eyes, is like a fracture that could lead to a full-blown failure.

> We don't have to be perfect to be a blessing. We are asked only to be real, trusting in Christ's perfection to cover our imperfection.
>
> *Gigi Graham Tchividjian*

In addition to making a mistake, your spouse fears having to compromise standards. And if you don't already know it, your spouse's standards are high. Your spouse aims high—in big things and little things. The Careful Spouse has standards about how the house should be cleaned (and remain clean), standards about how a car should be driven, and standards about how money should be handled. Of course, there are standards about character and integrity. In fact, your partner has standards about nearly everything. And if something or someone is causing your spouse to compromise those standards, it sends the Evaluator into a reactive mode. Your spouse likely becomes hypercritical and extremely moody.

> Aim for success, not perfection. Never give up your right to be wrong, because then you will lose the ability to learn new things and move forward with your life.
>
> *David M. Burns*

Another fear your Careful Spouse has is being misunderstood. Your spouse worries that you don't know what he or she really thinks or feels. In a conversation, your partner might sense that you are jumping to conclusions or reading something between the lines that was not intended, so the response may be, "You just don't understand me," or, "You don't get it." Of course, this fear translates into a condemning tone that may cause you to feel inadequate or dim-witted. But you can read this fear, at a deeper level, as a fear of losing your positive appraisal and your love.

How to Love a Careful Spouse

Everybody wants a happy marriage. And a happy marriage is the result of two people operating at the top of their game—where both spouses are functioning at their best, with the strengths from their inborn personalities in full play. With this in mind, here are a few specifics that will help you insure that your spouse can operate from the positive aspects of his or her God-given personality traits. It will also help you honor your spouse's Love Style.

Do What You Say You're Going to Do

Your Careful Spouse can be demanding. You know that. But it may help to know that these demands often stem from high levels of anxiety that surface when you don't "measure up" to your spouse's high standards. Of course, the standards may not be legitimate, but the anxiety your spouse experiences is real. In other words, your spouse feels extremely apprehensive when you break a promise or fail to meet deadlines or goals. If you say you're going to have the front closet cleaned out before the weekend and Friday night arrives and it's still not done, your spouse begins to feel like you're not trustworthy. The Evaluator wonders what other projects you're failing to do. The anxiety climbs, and the tension in your marriage mounts.

Of course, the human tendency is to push back on the seemingly unreasonable expectations of a spouse—about how the lawn should be mowed, when the bills are paid, how the pantry should be organized, and so on. But if you can stomach it, we suggest that you do your best to follow through on your projects, big or small, in a way that you know will please your Careful Spouse.

> The best proof of love is trust.
>
> *Dr. Joyce Brothers*

When you do this, it will not only make your spouse feel more loved, but it will also lower your partner's anxiety level about you in general—and that goes a long way in helping your spouse relax the high standards.

By the way, you can also help your spouse relax the standards for perfection by keeping your partner informed of your progress. Simply saying something like, "I'm making great progress on that project you wanted me to do. It's coming along really well." A comment like that lightens the load of an Evaluator. It helps the Careful Spouse breathe easier and feel more comfortable.

> Have patience with all things, but chiefly have patience with yourself. Do not lose courage in considering your own imperfections but instantly set about remedying them—every day begin the task anew.
>
> *Saint Francis de Sales*

So, let's make this clear. If you have a pattern of breaking your promises, you can better love your Careful Spouse when you not only follow through on what you say, but also when you accomplish projects at a level that makes your spouse happy. Few things make your Careful Spouse feel more loved than meeting the high standard.

Provide Stability

If you want more peace and joy in your marriage, if you want to make sure your Careful Spouse's needs are getting met, provide stability. Your spouse loves it. The Evaluator needs a sense of order in life to operate at the top of their game. The more order and stability you help to provide, the more loving your spouse will be toward you.

How can you do this? Begin by respecting the daily routines. For example, your spouse may like to begin the day by reading the paper over breakfast—without being interrupted for ten minutes or so. Take note. Maybe it's that last sip of coffee or perhaps it's when the fork is placed upside down on the plate. You can rest assured that your Careful Spouse gives a sign that his or her routine is complete. You may have to bite your tongue to respect the ritual, but if you do, you'll have a happier spouse on your hands.

You can also provide more stability to your partner's world by working to keep the schedule. This means doing your best to keep from springing last-minute requests or announcements that force the Careful Spouse to reorganize the plans without warning. If you're a last-minute kind of person with an Optimist Love Style, you'll need to adapt as best you can to meet this need, but we promise that it will pay off.

Stroke the Ego and Don't Make Fun

We'll say it straight: Your spouse is sensitive. Your spouse cringes at the thought of being poked fun at or ridiculed—especially in front of others. Everyone with an Evaluator Love Style will do almost anything to avoid this kind of embarrassment. If you are one who likes to send a little message now and then by joking around with a sarcastic comment, we want to caution you. This will shut down your spouse, and it won't help your message get through, either. The greatest fear of Evaluators is criticism of their work because they identify so closely with the quality of their work.

Your spouse takes life pretty seriously and wants support and encouragement. You may hear your Careful Spouse say it out loud: "Don't make fun of me." Now, if you have an Optimist Love Style, you're likely to tease back and laugh it up. Not your spouse. Lay off the sarcastic comments, even if they are said in fun.

Instead, let your Careful Spouse know just how much you support him or her. Ask questions like, "What can I do that would be most helpful for you right now?" Wow! That will get your partner's attention. Or say, "I want you to know that I'll do whatever I can to help you get through this project. Just let me know." Now you've provided the Evaluator with a solid foundation of support. With that in place, you can gently ease into your critique. "By the way, can I ask you something? I know you were trying to be helpful at the dinner party last night when you told Susan that her soup could have used some cumin, but do you think it came off

> The realization that I didn't have to be perfect strengthened my faith.
>
> *John Olerud*

that way?" This approach is far better than saying (especially in public), "Well, guess who needs to have their own cooking show?" The more gentle approach allows your spouse to hear the critique without working so hard to dodge the sarcastic darts. Others can handle sarcasm. Not your spouse. You can love your partner better by keeping this in mind.

Provide Space and Quiet

Your Careful Spouse needs to have breathing room, a place for quiet contemplation. Your partner needs a space that is off-limits to others. The Evaluator doesn't like you or anyone else messing with stuff. Careful Spouses don't want you borrowing "their" stapler. "You need to get your own," they might say to you. Picking up a favorite pen and discovering that it's noticeably sticky drives them crazy. "Who's been messing with my stuff?" they'll ask. Your spouse doesn't want you, your kids, your friends, your babysitter, or anyone else using his computer, his desk, his whatever. As we said, your spouse needs space to be free from noise, chatter, and commotion.

By the way, this applies to more than physical space. Your spouse needs emotional space as well. The Careful

Spouse doesn't like you to ask questions like an investigative reporter. Instead, allow your partner to tell you about the day as the evening unfolds, in his own time. If you get the sense that something is weighing on your spouse, you'll want to stay away from asking, "What's wrong with you?" Instead, say something like, "I'm guessing you feel bad, and I want you to know that I'm here when you feel like talking about it." This gives your spouse breathing room to talk without feeling smothered.

> Have no fear of perfection—you'll never reach it.
>
> *Salvador Dali*

To better love your Careful Spouse, you need to balance his or her need to be supported with the need for space. After all, because your spouse is hardwired for your support as well as space, it can be confusing—especially if you are an Encouraging Spouse whose support is typically about as subtle as a marching band.

How do you convey support while still giving the Evaluator space? In a word, *carefully*. That's what your spouse appreciates most. It's what makes the Careful Spouse feel loved. Your spouse wants a careful approach that doesn't ride roughshod over feelings yet doesn't stay so far removed that you become aloof. You need to think in terms of the middle ground on the emotional front—and stay clear of his or her "stuff."

Keep Your Marriage Thank-Tank Full

The "response threshold" is what researchers use to measure the degree of mess or disorder that must exist before one spouse in a marriage is sufficiently bothered to perform a task that's not being done by the other spouse. It could be anything from emptying the trash to filling up the gas tank in the car. Individuals with low response thresholds for a specific task are moved to perform the task earlier than those who have a higher threshold. In your marriage, it's bound to be your Careful Spouse who steps in first.

For example, if your spouse is disturbed when the garbage in the kitchen trashcan approaches the rim, but it doesn't bother you until the trash spills onto the floor, your spouse will take out the trash before you are moved to do so. If the difference in your tolerance levels is great enough, you will never empty the trash, because your Careful Spouse will always take care of it before it bothers you, possibly before you ever even notice the garbage.

If one partner's threshold level consistently is lower than the other's, then that first partner will take on more projects around the house. And here's the clincher: Regardless of who does what and how often, the critical factor found in successful marriages is that this work is genuinely appreciated—that gratitude is expressed frequently and genuinely.

> What is important to a relationship is a harmony of emotional roles.
>
> *Mira Komarovsky*

How are you doing on this front with your Careful Spouse? If you feel you could express more often your gratitude for specific (if not compulsive) acts of service, we encourage you to do just that. Anyone with an Evaluator Love Style thrives on this kind of appreciation.

Your Careful Spouse Feels Most Loved ...
When you make every effort to do
things right, while providing ongoing
support and a stable life together.

How to Stay Healthy with a Careful Spouse

One of the most important things you will ever do for your marriage is to stay healthy and strong yourself. If you don't take care of yourself, your marriage will suffer. So here are a few practical ways of doing just that—when married to an Evaluator.

Find Your Own Space

We've noted that your spouse needs private space where things aren't touched and everything can be "perfect." Well, if you're not inclined to be organized and neat like your spouse, then you need to create a space where you and your spouse agree that you have permission to be as sloppy and disorganized as you like.

> Assert your right to make a few mistakes. If people can't accept your imperfections, that's their fault.
>
> *David M. Burns*

This might be a project room, a desk, a portion of the garage, or the corner of the basement.

Not only do you need to create this space if you don't already have it, but also you need to let your Careful Spouse know that it's off-limits to any organizing compulsions. The point is that, just as you respect the space of your Careful Spouse, your partner needs to respect your right to a space that is your own as well.

Give Up the Guilt Trip

Your partner's high standards are ripe with opportunities to make you feel guilty. More than most spouses, you will inevitably drop the ball and disappoint your partner because you are human. And no human can always measure up to exceedingly high standards. It's just not possible. That's where the feelings of guilt enter in.

Of course, there is a huge difference between true guilt and false guilt. Not measuring up to unrealistically high standards results in false guilt and regret — the kind nobody deserves to feel. "Regret is an appalling waste of energy," says writer Katherine Mansfield. "You can't build on it. It's only good for wallowing in."

> Love comes when manipulation stops; when you think more about the other person than about his or her reactions to you. When you dare to reveal yourself fully. When you dare to be vulnerable.
>
> *Dr. Joyce Brothers*

So be kind to yourself and take note of your self-punishment. Don't waste another minute wallowing in regret and guilt that you didn't deserve to feel in the first place. How? By seeing how irrational it is. True guilt is based on solid facts, like breaking a known law or a moral code. False guilt is based on feelings. That's all. You assume that because you *feel* guilty you *are* guilty. But that's not the case. If your spouse is handing out free tickets for an undeserved guilt trip, kindly decline. You and your marriage will be better for it.

Build Yourself into the Routine

Because your spouse lives by schedule, ritual, and routine, you can use this to your advantage to get the kind of time you want with your Careful Spouse. For example, your spouse may like to linger for a few minutes at the dinner table after the kids have scattered. Resist your temptation to clear the plates or read the paper and make this your "together time." If this doesn't work, consider the morning rituals. Maybe it's after a morning run over a glass of juice. You get the idea. All you have to do is find a ritual that is already present in your spouse's life and carve out some space within it.

Once you do this, your Careful Spouse won't want to miss out on it. Your partner is a creature of habit. As long as you're consistent, your spouse will be too.

Maintain Your Sense of Humor

Because your Careful Spouse is prone to moodiness and takes life pretty seriously, it can dampen your natural sense of humor. While he or she may not be yukking it up with you all the time, your spouse appreciates your wit. The more merriment you can bring into the Careful Spouse's life, the better your marriage will be. Essayist and biographer Agnes Repplier, who was known for her common sense and good judgment, said, "We cannot really love anybody with whom we never laugh." It's true. The more you laugh together, the more loving you become.

> I am careful not to confuse excellence with perfection. Excellence, I can reach for; perfection is God's business.
>
> *Michael J. Fox*

Your sense of humor will also help you maintain your objectivity when you feel taken in by your Careful Spouse's perfectionist ways. It will help you step back and see the situation more clearly (and help you avoid the false guilt that perfectionist expectations often stirs). Let's say you spill a few muffin crumbs on the floor that your Careful Spouse just swept. "Look what you did!" your spouse exclaims. You might be inclined to cringe. But, truly, it's not the end of the world. You can say with a smile and a kiss, "I think we'll survive." The little glint in your eye as you wipe it up sends a light-hearted message to your spouse. More importantly, it helps you maintain your objectivity and remain calm.

Laughter has been called a tranquilizer with no side effects. It washes away stress and keeps you unruffled. To paraphrase Henry Ward Beecher, "A marriage without a sense of humor is like a wagon without springs—jolted by every pebble in the road."

> A diamond with a flaw is worth more than a pebble without imperfections.
>
> *Chinese proverb*

For Reflection and Discussion

1. What is it like being married to a spouse with this Love Style? In other words, what are the benefits and what are the challenges of living with this particular style? Be specific.

2. Now that you have a clearer understanding of what makes your spouse feel most loved, what is one thing you can do in the next day or so to do just that? Which of the suggestions in this chapter seem most challenging to you when it comes to loving your spouse? Why?

3. When it comes to staying healthy with your spouse's Love Style, which suggestion in this chapter do you personally feel could benefit you the most? How, in specific terms, can you begin putting it into practice?

WORKBOOK EXERCISE
for the Spouse of an Evaluator

If you're electing to use the optional his/her interactive workbooks, you'll want to turn to the exercise designed specifically for you to apply this chapter to your marriage. It contains several brief exercises that are sure to make this information come alive in your relationship.

GETTING THE LOVE YOU WANT

The meeting of two personalities is like the contact of two chemical substances; if there is any reaction, both are transformed.

Carl Gustav Jung

VIOLET BAILEY AND her fiancé Samuel Booth were strolling through the English countryside in 1941, deeply in love. A diamond engagement ring sparkled on Violet's finger—her most treasured possession.

But, as can happen with couples, something was said that hurt the other's feelings and an argument ensued, then escalated. At its worst point, Violet became so angry she pulled the diamond engagement ring from her finger, drew back her arm, and hurled the treasured possession with all her might into the field. The ring sailed through the air, fell to the ground, and nestled under the grass in such a way that it was impossible to see.

Violet and Samuel eventually made up. Their argument, both agreed, was foolish. Desperate to recover their lost ring, they walked and walked through that field hunting for it. They never found it.

Two months later, they were married. They had a child

and eventually a grandson. Part of their family lore was the story of the lost engagement ring. Everyone knew about it, even decades later.

Violet and Samuel grew old together, and in 1993 Samuel died. Fifteen years passed, but the ring was not forgotten. One day Violet's grandson got an idea. Perhaps he could find his grandmother's ring with a metal detector. With a newly purchased detector in hand, he went to the field where Violet had hurled her treasured possession 67 years earlier. He turned on the machine and began to crisscross the field, waving the detector over the grass. After two hours of searching, he finally found what he was looking for.

> Love is the master key which opens the gates of happiness.
> *Oliver Wendell Holmes*

Later, with immense joy and pride, the grandson placed the diamond ring into the hand of his astonished grandmother Violet. The treasured possession had finally come home.[12]

Can you imagine finally discovering what you've been hoping to find for more than six decades? The story, of course, is bittersweet. While the ring was found, Samuel didn't get to finally place that lost ring on her finger. Violet found what she was looking for, but most would say it was much too late.

Don't let the same thing happen in your marriage. We're not talking about losing a ring, of course. We're talking about something far more precious. We're talking about losing days that turn into years where you don't get the love you want.

We've written this book and created the online L.O.V.E. Style Assessment to insure that this doesn't happen to you. We conclude by underscoring exactly what this experience of discovering your unique Love Styles can do for your relationship. Specifically, we leave you with two important points.

Nobody Lives by a Label

We told you at the outset, but it bears repeating. We've presented the four Love Styles in ways that are intentionally simplistic and somewhat exaggerated. The style descriptions and characteristics serve best as jumping-off points for better understanding the unique set of nuanced and blended Love Styles with which each of you are hardwired. You may be 70 percent a Take-Charge Spouse and 30 percent an Encouraging Spouse. You may be any combination of all four styles. Everyone is unique.

We don't expect you to agree with every portion or every point that focuses on you and your Love Style. You're likely to agree with some areas and disagree with others. That's how it should be.

Again, the point of this experience is not to put anybody in a box or give anybody a label that can always sum them up. When you consider the four quadrants of the L.O.V.E. Model, think in terms of how much of your personality is shaped by whether you are Project-Oriented or People-Oriented. And how much you're shaped by whether you are Fast-Paced or Slow-Paced. Of course, the online assessment may show you to be nearly right in the middle of either one of these two dimensions. That's why we encourage you to let the online assessment make this journey for you much more personally relevant.

Keep the Big Picture in View

Understanding your two unique Love Styles is simply a tool for helping you both get the love you want —

without having to wait. You see, by taking a deep look at your inner hardwiring for love, we hope we've helped you enter into each other's worlds. We hope we've helped you see what your spouse fears in your relationship.

> Love is the condition in which the happiness of another person is essential to your own.
>
> *Robert Heinlein*

We hope we've helped you know what to expect. We hope we've shown you how you can be a better spouse with your particular hardwiring and how you can better love your spouse when you compare and contrast your styles.

In short, we hope we've given you a tool for empathy —that capacity to see the world from each other's perspective. Of course, there's more to empathy than understanding personalities. We're also shaped by life experiences, family backgrounds, cultural customs, and so on. But accurately understanding the intricacies of each other's personalities goes a long way toward making mutual empathy profoundly impact your marriage.

And why does this matter? Because empathy, no matter what your Love Style, is at the heart of every healthy marriage. It's what allows you to walk in each other's

> Mutual empathy is the great unsung human gift.
>
> *Jean Baker Miller*

shoes without stepping on each other's toes. Hundreds of research studies have pointed to the immeasurable value of empathy in marriage. Now you have one of the greatest means for enjoying it in yours.

Albert Schweitzer was a musician and physician who won the Nobel Peace Prize in 1952. This is the message he left for us when he died: "I don't know what your destiny will be, but one thing I do know: the only ones among you who will be really happy are those who have sought and found how to serve."

> We come to love not by finding a perfect person, but by learning to see an imperfect person perfectly.
>
> *Sam Keen*

That's the message we leave you with in this book. Your level of happiness in your marriage is dependent upon how well you serve one another, by giving your spouse—whether he or she be Take-Charge, Encouraging, Devoted, Careful, or any combination of all four—the kind of love they need and desire.

APPENDIXES

APPENDIX A:
Comparing the Four Love Styles

	L	O	V	E
	Leader: The Take-Charge Spouse	**Optimist:** The Encouraging Spouse	**Validator:** The Devoted Spouse	**Evaluator:** The Careful Spouse
Title				
Descriptor	Doer	Talker	Watcher	Thinker
Motivator	Power	Popularity	Peace	Perfection
Need	Control	Pleasure	Harmony	Excellence
Fear	Failure	Rejection	Conflict	Mediocrity
Satisfaction	Save Time	Win Approval	Gain Loyalty	Achieve Quality
Motto	If it's worth doing–do it now	If it's worth doing–make it fun	If it's worth doing–we'll do it together	If it's worth doing–it's worth doing right
At Best	Goal-oriented Focused Self-confident Visionary Hard working	Fun-loving Positive Persuasive Sociable Encouraging	Loyal Agreeable Thoughtful Tolerant Nurturing	Orderly Conscientious Scheduled Purposeful Factual
At Worst	Stubborn Insensitive Annoyed Hot-tempered Domineering	Avoids conflict Dramatic Off task Procrastinates Forgetful	Introverted Indecisive Resists change Unenthusiastic Pleaser	Obsessive Critical Moody Suspicious Rigid
Definition of Love	Being intentional and active about building our future together	Being attentive and giving each other affection and acceptance	Being reassured that we are on the same team	Being thorough, accurate, and true to our commitments and standards
Approach to Conflict	Let's find a quick solution.	Let's work together to solve this	Let me think this through on my own first?	Let me consider this from every angle.
Perspective	"The glass is half full—as long as I maintain control of it."	"The glass is half full—and contains more than you think."	"The glass is half empty—but we'll manage together."	"The glass is half empty—and probably leaking."

APPENDIX B:
Sample Online L.O.V.E. Style Report

Below and on the next page are four sample pages to show you what the online L.O.V.E. Style Report will look like. The full report is twelve pages long, full of helpful information on how you are wired to love and how you can use that knowledge to enhance your relationship with your spouse. To engage with this valuable resource, visit www.RealRelationships.com.

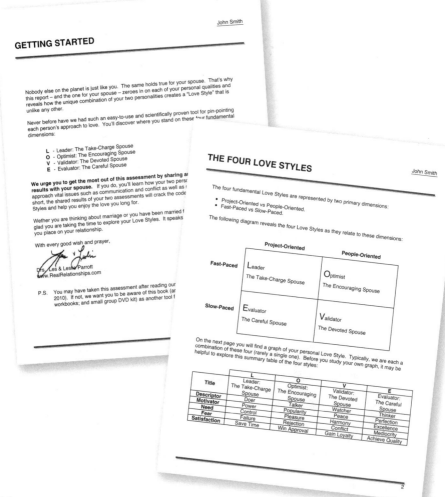

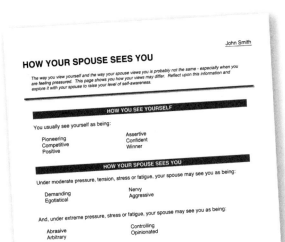

HOW YOUR SPOUSE SEES YOU

The way you view yourself and the way your spouse views you is probably not the same - especially when you are feeling pressured. This page shows you how your views may differ. Reflect upon this information and explore it with your spouse to raise your level of self-awareness.

HOW YOU SEE YOURSELF

You usually see yourself as being:

Pioneering
Competitive
Positive

Assertive
Confident
Winner

HOW YOUR SPOUSE SEES YOU

Under moderate pressure, tension, stress or fatigue, your spouse may see you as being:

Demanding
Egotistical

Nervy
Aggressive

And, under extreme pressure, stress or fatigue, your spouse may see you as being:

Abrasive
Arbitrary

Controlling
Opinionated

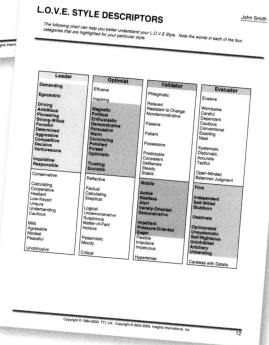

L.O.V.E. STYLE DESCRIPTORS

The following chart can help you better understand your L.O.V.E Style. Note the words in each of the four categories that are highlighted for your particular style.

Leader	Optimist	Validator	Evaluator
Demanding	Effusive	Phlegmatic	Evasive
Egocentric	Inspiring	Relaxed	Worrisome
Driving	Magnetic	Resistant to Change	Careful
Ambitious	Political	Nondemonstrative	Dependent
Pioneering	Enthusiastic		Cautious
Strong-Willed	Demonstrative	Passive	Conventional
Forceful	Persuasive		Exacting
Determined	Warm	Patient	Neat
Aggressive	Convincing		
Competitive	Polished	Possessive	Systematic
Decisive	Poised		Diplomatic
Venturesome	Optimistic	Predictable	Accurate
		Consistent	Tactful
Inquisitive	Trusting	Deliberate	
Responsible	Sociable	Steady	Open-Minded
		Stable	Balanced Judgment
Conservative	Reflective		
		Mobile	Firm
Calculating	Factual		
Cooperative	Calculating	Active	Independent
Hesitant	Skeptical	Restless	Self-Willed
Low-Keyed		Alert	Stubborn
Unsure	Logical	Variety-Oriented	
Undemanding	Undemonstrative	Demonstrative	Obstinate
Cautious	Suspicious		
	Matter-of-Fact	Impatient	Opinionated
Mild	Incisive	Pressure-Oriented	Unsystematic
Agreeable		Eager	Self-Righteous
Modest	Pessimistic	Flexible	Uninhibited
Peaceful	Moody	Impulsive	Arbitrary
		Impetuous	Unbending
Unobtrusive	Critical		
		Hypertense	Careless with Details

NOTES

1. Interestingly, the one area that seems to devote an inordinate amount of effort in understanding personality as it relates to a broad aspect of life is leadership and managerial preferences in the workplace. The Blake-Mouton Grid and McGregor's Theory X and Theory Y are good examples.

2. Of course, genes do not account for all of personality, just the seeds of it. Environment also plays a significant role. Scientists' unwieldy name for this exchange is "evocative gene-environment correlations," so called because people's genetic makeup is thought to bring forth particular reactions from others, which in turn influences their personalities.

3. Robert Plomin, John C. DeFries, Gerald E. McClearn, Peter McGuffin, *Behavioral Genetics*, 5th ed. (New York: Worth Publishers, 2008).

4. Robert Plomin, "Behavioral Genetics and Personality Change," *Journal of Personality*, 58, no.1 / (March 1990): 191–220.

5. Which is why DNA left at a crime scene can be strongly linked to one individual.

6. Bjorn Carey, "Ant School: The First Formal Classroom Found in Nature." Posted january 13, 2006. www.foxnews.com/story/0,2933,181364,00.html.

7. Leviticus 16:10: "But the goat chosen by lot as the scapegoat shall be presented alive before the Lord to be used for making atonement by sending it into the desert as a scapegoat."

8. Ephesians 4:15.

9. E. Stanley Jones, *The Way* (New York: Doubleday, 1978).

10. Deborah Tannen, *You Just Don't Understand: Women and Men in Conversation*. New York: Ballantine Books, 1990.

11. E. Giltay, *Archives of General Psychiatry* 61 (November 2004): 1126–1135, reported at www.foxnews.com/story/0,2933,137312,00.html.

12. "It Wasn't All Bad." *The Week*. Posted February 15, 2008. Page 4.

ACKNOWLEDGMENTS

Thanks to ...

Zondervan. Dudley Delffs, Sandy Vander Zicht, Becky Philpott, Tom Dean, Joyce Ondersma, Jackie Aldridge, and everyone else at ZPH who pulled together to make this book come to life. This marks another in a long line of projects we've done together and we are so grateful to share this history with you.

The Unity Media Group in Boise, Idaho. Michael Boerner and his creative team, including Ken Holsinger, Jason Behrman, Debbie Kling, Rich Granberry, and everybody else at Unity, is a powerhouse of added value to everything they touch. The innovation you've provided in making the personalized coaching we're now able to do online with this content is magical.

Evan and Ellena Johnson at Imigri in Seattle, Washington. We can't say thanks enough for your generosity in offering your talents to the cover design and to the small group DVD production that accompanies this book. Your fingerprints are all over this effort.

Rodney Cox, of Ministry Insights International in Scottsdale, Arizona. You are such a good friend and your tender teaching of these principles made this project possible. It simply would not exist without your generous spirit and kind encouragement.

Ron Price of Price Associates in Boise, Idaho. Your expertise in showing us how to "put the cookies on the bottom shelf" when it comes to unpacking a sophisticated personality assessment is a true gift.

Sealy Yates of Yates and Yates in Orange, California. We never take you for granted. You do more for us than any authors could ever ask. We are so grateful to have you in our corner. And we're even more grateful to count you as a good friend. We'll never forget our 25th anniversary because of you!

Church Communication Network, which is located virtually everywhere (literally). Bill and Bettina Dallas, and colleagues such as Jay Mitchell, Terry Rouch, Johanna Cabrera, Sarah Schleiger, Deb Fahey, Deb Layman, Kim Wood, and Patti Christensen, make the reach of this effort unfathomable. We are so glad to be part of the team you are on.

Janice Lundquist in Chicago, Illinois. We don't know how you do it from half a continent away, but you consistently pull the details of our life together—week after week, and year after year. And you do so with such grace. We can't imagine this ride without you.

Friends like Mark and Stephanie Cole, Rich and Linda Simons, George and Liz Toles, Tim and Britney Gaydos, Kevin and Robin Small, James and Nancy Smith, Steve and Jewell Harmon, Steve and Thanne Moore, Kevin and Kathy Lunn, Mark and Candi Brown, Doug and Margo Engberg, Loran and Brenda Lichty, Jeff and Stacy Kemp, Ken and Stacey Coleman, Mark and Geri Bottles, and Steve and Barb Uhlmann. You all offered feedback and advice in various ways and at various stages during this project. We are grateful for that—and blessed to know you as friends.

Thank you all.

Les & Leslie Parrott
Seattle, Washington

About the Authors

Drs. Les and Leslie Parrott are founders and codirectors of the Center for Relationship Development at Seattle Pacific University (SPU), a groundbreaking program dedicated to teaching the basics of good relationships. Les Parrott is a professor of psychology at SPU, and Leslie is a marriage and family therapist at SPU. The Parrotts are authors of *Becoming Soul Mates, Your Time-Starved Marriage, Love Talk, The Parent You Want to Be*, and the Gold Medallion Award-winning *Saving Your Marriage Before It Starts*. The Parrotts have been featured on *Oprah, CBS This Morning*, CNN, and *The View*, and in *USA Today* and the *New York Times*. They are also frequent guest speakers and have written for a variety of magazines. The Parrotts' radio program, *Love Talk*, can be heard on stations throughout North America. Their website, RealRelationships.com, features more than one thousand free video-on-demand pieces answering relationship questions. Les and Leslie live in Seattle, Washington, with their two sons.

Love Talk

Speak Each Other's Language Like You Never Have Before

Drs. Les and Leslie Parrott

A breakthrough discovery in communication for transforming love relationships.

Over and over, couples consistently name "improved communication" as the greatest need in their relationships. *Love Talk*, by acclaimed relationship experts Drs. Les and Leslie Parrott, is a deep yet simple plan full of new insights that will revolutionize communication in love relationships.

In this no-nonsense book, "psychobabble" is translated into easy-to-understand language that clearly teaches you what you need to do — and not do — in order to speak each other's language like you never have before.

Love Talk includes:

- The Love Talk Indicator, a free personalized online assessment (a $30.00 value) to help you determine your unique talk style
- The Secret to Emotional Connection
- Charts and sample conversations
- The most important conversation you'll ever have
- A short course on Communication 101
- Appendix on Practical Help for the "Silent Partner"

Two softcover his and hers workbooks are full of lively exercises and enlightening self-tests that help couples apply what they are learning about communication directly to their relationships.

Hardcover, Jacketed 978-0-310-24596-4

Also Available:

978-0-310-26214-5	Love Talk	Audio CD, Abridged
978-0-310-26467-5	Love Talk Curriculum Kit	DVD
978-0-310-81047-6	Love Talk Starters	Mass Market
978-0-310-26212-1	Love Talk Workbook for Men	Softcover
978-0-310-26213-8	Love Talk Workbook for Women	Softcover

The Parent You Want to Be

Who You Are Matters More Than What You Do

Drs. Les and Leslie Parrott

Being a parent is the most important calling you will ever have — with the emphasis on being. This parenting book is unlike any other: it's a step-by-step guide to selecting and modeling the very traits that you want your child to have. Because, as the authors explain, parenting is more about who you are than what you do.

Children long to be like their parents. That's the secret behind this method of choosing your top traits — your "intentional traits" — and projecting them consistently.

What is the single most important question you can ask yourself as a parent? Find out in this book. You'll also learn the three-step method to avoid becoming the parent you don't want to be ... how to hear what your child isn't saying ... the single best way to teach a child patience ... and much more.

Written in short, designed-for-busy-parent chapters, with self-tests and discussion questions, this book helps you select your top traits and make them stick. Filled with encouragement, inspiring examples, and warm personal stories from their own experiences with their children, this book offers the Parrotts' revolutionary road map to parenting success.

Hardcover, Jacketed: 978-0-310-27245-8
Audio CD, Unabridged: 978-0-310-27977-8
Audio Download, Unabridged: 978-0-310-27978-5

Pick up a copy today at your favorite bookstore!

ZONDERVAN®
.com

You Matter More Than You Think

What a Woman Needs to Know about the Difference She Makes

Dr. Leslie Parrott

Am I making a difference?
Does my life matter?

"How can I make a difference when some days I can't even find my keys?" asks award-winning author Leslie Parrott. "I've never been accused of being methodical, orderly, or linear. So when it came to considering my years on this planet, I did so without a sharpened pencil and a pad of paper. Instead, I walked along Discovery Beach, just a few minutes from our home in Seattle.

"Strange, though. All I seemed to ever bring home from my walks on the beach were little pieces of sea glass. Finding these random pieces eventually became a fixation. And, strangely, with each piece I collected, I felt a sense of calm. What could this mean? What was I to discover from this unintentional collection?"

In this poignant and vulnerable book, Leslie shows you how each hodgepodge piece of your life, no matter how haphazard, represents a part of what you do and who you are. While on the surface, none of these pieces may seem to make a terribly dramatic impact, Leslie will show you how they are your life and how when they are collected into a jar — a loving human heart— they become a treasure.

Hardcover, Jacketed: 978-0-310-24598-8
Softcover: 978-0-310-32497-3

Pick up a copy today at your favorite bookstore!

Trading Places

The Secret to the Marriage You Want

Drs. Les and Leslie Parrott

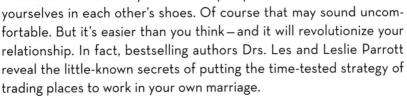

DRS. LES & LESLIE PARROTT

To understand your spouse you've got to walk in his or her shoes.

Ever feel like you're stepping on each other's toes? Then maybe it's time you put yourselves in each other's shoes. Of course that may sound uncomfortable. But it's easier than you think—and it will revolutionize your relationship. In fact, bestselling authors Drs. Les and Leslie Parrott reveal the little-known secrets of putting the time-tested strategy of trading places to work in your own marriage.

In this book, chock-full of practical helps and tips you've never thought of, you'll learn the three-step-strategy to trading places and, as a result, you're sure to:

- Increase your levels of passion
- Bolster your commitment
- Eliminate nagging
- Short-circuit conflict
- Double your laughter
- Forgive more quickly
- Talk more intimately

This book also features a powerful, free online assessment that instantly improves your inclination to trade places.

Most couples never discover the rewards of trading places. For example, did you know it's the quickest way to get your own needs met? It's true! And Les and Leslie show you how. They also disclose exactly how trading places improves your conversations and how it's guaranteed to fire up your sex life. Truly, your love life and your entire marriage will never be the same after you learn the intimate dance of trading places.

Also available in unabridged audio CD edition

Softcover: 978-0-310-32779-0

The Complete Guide to Marriage Mentoring

Connecting Couples to Build Better Marriages

Drs. Les and Leslie Parrott

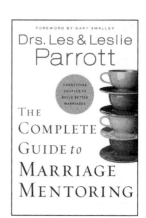

A comprehensive resource to help churches build a thriving marriage mentoring program.

Les and Leslie Parrott are passionate about how marriage mentoring can transform couples, families, and entire congregations. *The Complete Guide to Marriage Mentoring* includes life-changing insights and essential skills for

- Preparing engaged and newlywed couples
- Maximizing marriages from good to great
- Repairing marriages in distress

Practical guidelines help mentors and couples work together as a team, agree on outcomes, and develop skills for the marriage mentoring process. Appendixes offer a wealth of additional resources and tools. An exhaustive resource for marriage mentorship in any church setting, this guide also includes insights from interviews with church leaders and marriage mentors from around the country.

> "The time is ripe for marriage mentoring, and this book is exactly what we need."
>
> — Gary Smalley, author of *The DNA of Relationships*

Hardcover, Printed 978-0-310-27046-1

Also Available:

978-0-310-27047-8	51 Creative Ideas for Marriage Mentors	Softcover
978-0-310-27110-9	Complete Resource Kit for Marriage Mentoring, The	Curriculum Kit
978-0-310-27165-9	Marriage Mentor Training Manual for Husbands	Softcover
978-0-310-27125-3	Marriage Mentor Training Manual for Wives	Softcover

Pick up a copy today at your favorite bookstore!

ZONDERVAN®
.com

Saving Your Marriage Before It Starts

Seven Questions to Ask Before — and After —You Marry

Drs. Les and Leslie Parrott

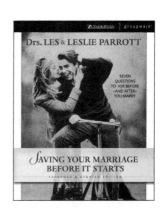

A trusted marriage resource for engaged and newlywed couples is now expanded and updated.

With more than 500,000 copies in print, *Saving Your Marriage Before It Starts* has become the gold standard for helping today's engaged and newlywed couples build a solid foundation for lifelong love.

This expanded and updated edition of *Saving Your Marriage Before It Starts* has been honed by ten years of feedback, professional experience, research, and insight, making this tried-and-true resource better than ever. Specifically designed to meet the needs of today's couples, this book equips readers for a lifelong marriage before it even starts.

The men's and women's workbooks include self-tests and exercises sure to bring about personal insight and help you apply what you learn. The seven-session DVD features the Parrotts' lively presentation as well as real-life couples, making this a tool you can use "right out of the box." Two additional sessions for second marriages are also included. The unabridged audio CD is read by the authors.

The Curriculum Kit includes DVD with Leader's Guide, hardcover book, workbooks for men and women, and *Saving Your Second Marriage Before It Starts* workbooks for men and women. All components, except for DVD, are also sold separately.

Curriculum Kit: 978-0-310-27180-2

Also Available:
978-0-310-26210-7   Saving Your Marriage Before It Starts   Audio CD, Unabridged
978-0-310-26565-8   Saving Your Marriage Before It Starts Workbook for Men   Softcover
978-0-310-26564-1   Saving Your Marriage Before It Starts Workbook for Women   Softcover
978-0-310-27585-5   Saving Your Second Marriage Before It Starts Workbook for Women   Softcover
978-0-310-27584-8   Saving Your Second Marriage Before It Starts Workbook for Men   Softcover

I Love You More

How Everyday Problems Can Strengthen Your Marriage

Drs. Les and Leslie Parrott

How to make the thorns in your marriage come up roses.

The big and little annoyances in your marriage are actually opportunities to deepen your love for each other. Relationship experts and award-winning authors Les and Leslie Parrott believe that your personal quirks and differences — where you squeeze the toothpaste tube, how you handle money — can actually help draw you together provided you handle them correctly.

Turn your marriage's prickly issues into opportunities to love each other more as you learn how to:

- build intimacy while respecting personal space
- tap the power of a positive marriage attitude
- replace boredom with fun, irritability with patience, busyness with time together, debt with a team approach to your finances … and much, much more.

Plus — get an inside look at the very soul of your marriage, and how connecting with God can connect you to each other in ways you never dreamed.

Softcover: 978-0-310-25738-7

Also Available:
978-0-310-26582-5	I Love You More Curriculum Kit	DVD
978-0-310-26275-6	I Love You More Workbook for Men	Softcover
978-0-310-26276-3	I Love You More Workbook for Women	Softcover

Pick up a copy today at your favorite bookstore!

ZONDERVAN®
.com

Your Time-Starved Marriage

How to Stay Connected at the Speed of Life

Drs. Les and Leslie Parrott

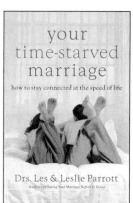

This is not a book about being more productive — it's a book about being more connected as a couple. In *Your Time-Starved Marriage*, Drs. Les and Leslie Parrott show how you can create a more fulfilling relationship with time — and with each other.

The moments you miss together are gone forever. Irreplaceable. And yet, until now, there has not been a single book for couples on how to better manage and reclaim this priceless resource. The Parrotts show you how to take back the time you've been missing together — and maximize the moments you already have. *Your Time-Starved Marriage* shows you how to:

- relate to time in a new way as a couple
- understand two lies every time-starved couple so easily believes
- slay the "busyness" giant that threatens your relationship
- integrate your time-style with a step-by-step approach that helps you make more time together
- stop the "time bandits" that steal your minutes
- maximize mealtime, money time, and leisure time
- reclaim all the free time you've been throwing away

Your Time-Starved Marriage gives you tools to feed your time-starved relationship, allowing you to maximize the moments you have together and enjoy them more.

Hardcover, Jacketed: 978-0-310-24597-1

Also Available:

978-0-310-81053-7	Time Together	Hardcover, Jacketed
978-0-310-26885-7	Your Time-Starved Marriage	Audio CD, Unabridged
978-0-310-27103-1	Your Time-Starved Marriage Groupware DVD	DVD
978-0-310-27155-0	Your Time-Starved Marriage Workbook for Men	Softcover
978-0-310-26729-4	Your Time-Starved Marriage Workbook for Women	Softcover

Share Your Thoughts

With the Author: Your comments will be forwarded to the author when you send them to *zauthor@zondervan.com*.

With Zondervan: Submit your review of this book by writing to *zreview@zondervan.com*.

Free Online Resources at

www.zondervan.com

Zondervan AuthorTracker: Be notified whenever your favorite authors publish new books, go on tour, or post an update about what's happening in their lives at www.zondervan.com/authortracker.

Daily Bible Verses and Devotions: Enrich your life with daily Bible verses or devotions that help you start every morning focused on God. Visit www.zondervan.com/newsletters.

Free Email Publications: Sign up for newsletters on Christian living, academic resources, church ministry, fiction, children's resources, and more. Visit www.zondervan.com/newsletters.

Zondervan Bible Search: Find and compare Bible passages in a variety of translations at www.zondervanbiblesearch.com.

Other Benefits: Register yourself to receive online benefits like coupons and special offers, or to participate in research.

ZONDERVAN.com/
AUTHORTRACKER
follow your favorite authors